Weed Out

Building India upon Values

By

Toshan Nimai Das

Readers interested in the subject matter of the book are invited by the Ethiccraft Publication to correspond with its secretary at the following address:

386, Sant Nagar, East of Kailash,
New Delhi 110065, India

Website:

www.ethiccraftclub.org

Email:
info@ethiccraftclub.org

1st Printing in India: 5,000 Copies

ISBN 978-81-93992-14-2

Disclaimer: Weed Out is a work of fiction. Any resemblance to actual events or persons, living or dead, is entirely coincidental. The 1960's counter culture in USA and works of Swami Bhaktivedanta, however, are very real in this story.

Published & Printed by
Ethiccraft Publication

Reviews

- "Weed Out" is a thoughtful book. In order to enlighten and create awareness about the hazardous effects of addiction, this highly informative and inspiring book named on De-addiction as an asset for the youth.

  -Dr. P.B. Sharma, Vice Chancellor, Amity University Gurugram

- The book weed out is an aid to the youth. It will help the youth of the nation to become empowered to safeguard themselves from self-destructive practices and habits. I wholeheartedly appreciate such endeavors and I request all the students, youths, parents, faculty members, leaders of the society to read this book.

  - Manish Sisodia Deputy Chief Minister, Delhi

- The book "Weed Out" is a very thoughtful and pragmatic analysis of the prevalent situation of youth tormented by the menace of self-destructive addictions. The storyline of the book has the potency to behold the attention of the audience until the very end while very systematically elucidating the vicious network of addiction which retards the development of the youth. Such texts are the need of the hour.

  -Dr. Vivek Bindra, International Motivational Speaker, Business Consultant, and Life coach

• Author has been able to convey the message in a very beautiful manner. Conspiracy angle of foreign enemy countries to weaken India by taking its youth wing attracted towards drugs has also been well placed in the book. Overall, in my opinion, it is a very informative piece of work for the welfare of society. The writer has fulfilled his social duty by pinpointing the present serious problem of the nation in a very lucid manner. I really appreciate his work.

-Subodh Kumar Srivastava,
Retd. District and Sessions Judge.
At present:- President, District Consumer
Disputes Redressal Forum, Vaishali at
Hajipur

(Bihar).

About the Author

Toshan Nimai Das has a bachelor's degree in Engineering. He is a practicing monk. He regularly teaches practical wisdom at various colleges and in the corporate world. He has undertaken various software development projects for benefit of society.

The book is Dedicated to,
my beloved teachers,
family, and friends.

Acknowledgments

To my all mentors and colleagues, by whose support and guidance, I am writing this book.

To my family who has always encouraged and inspired me.

I would like to express my heartfelt gratitude to the whole team of Ethiccraft club for their valuable support in publishing this book. We sincerely wish them best for the drug awareness campaign.

I would like to especially thank Sriman Sundar Gopal Das, President of Ethiccraft club for extending a helping hand despite hectic engagements for this noble cause of spreading awareness about addiction.

I sincerely express my gratitude to Ms. Amala Reddie, Ms. Simran Paul, Ms. Oindrila Majumder, Ms. Komal Kumar, and Mr. Nirmal Punjabi, they have done valuable work of polishing this book by editing and proofreading it.

I thank Mr. Sushant Dhanwade for attractive cover design.

I offer my most profound gratitude to HH Radhanath Swami. His talk on the '12 steps program' given in 1989 helped to set the tone of this book.

I thank Mrs. Swati Thorat from Anti Narcotics cell and Mrs. Radhika Phadke from Cyber Security cell of Pune police for giving me their valuable time to know details about their cell operations and I also thank Dr. Rishabh Kumar Singh for sharing valuable information as a part of research work for this book.

Mr. Mangesh Karlekar and Mr. Manav Jogdev are gentle souls from Muktangan who graciously helped me to know details of their work at the rehabilitation center.

Prof. Jagadeeswaran and Mr. Sangharsh from FTII for their valuable feedback regarding this book.

Mr. Amit Tutika for adjusting my services, without his kind help it was not possible to finish this book start to end, within a short period of two months.

Many critics who took the pain to go through the book and gave me valuable feedback; every feedback has helped me to improve this book. I sincerely thank them all.

...Author

Foreword

During my long innings as teacher/academic administrator for 40 years, I have been sadly observing the growth of drug abuse on academic campuses. It is time to curb and take measures. It appears that some elements inimical to our motherland are pushing the drugs on our campuses to make our youth physically, mentally and emotionally weak.

Drug Addiction and substance abuse is a chronic, relapsing disease wherein the drug user compulsively spends time looking for and using an Illegal drug. Estimates indicate that there are around three million drug addicts in India.

"Weed Out" by Toshan Nimai Das is an educational story that helps one understands how the whole vicious cycle occurs through the two major characters in the book. Das has cleverly woven the fabric around two friends, one who fights the perpetrators of this menace and one who falls victim to them.

The effects of addiction on the mental, physical, emotional, social and spiritual well-being of youth are masterfully depicted. Also, this book shows how the victim comes out of the clutches of abuse to redemption.

A thought-provoking read for students, parents, and educators.

-Dr. G R.C Reddy
(Vice Chancellor, Sharda University, Greater Noida)

Contents

- Prologue 1

Part I

- Double Edged 6
- Life fizzled out 9
- Trapped 15
- I'll always miss you 21
- Life's Mission 26

Part II

- Sharanam 32
- 12 Steps of Escape 37
- He was Murdered 51
- The Wisdom of Yoga Sutras 57
- Swami in the Hippie Land 67

Part III

- Stealthy Route 84
- The Peddler's Story 90
- Intrusion 97
- The Walkathon 105
- Finish Her Off 118
- Tempt Fate 120
- The bleed India Plot 127
- Who is the Murderer? 133

Prologue

The sea felt so vast and turbulent, I sat there meditating in a calm mood, it was an unusually quiet afternoon. Each wave rushed towards the shore with great force and elegance. The turquoise waters seemed boundless. I appeared like a small creature, powerless, just insignificant in front of it. I perceived the natural forces to be so strong almost impossible to forego their influence. Similar to those forces were the strong unseen ropes of limitations which I felt were binding us all humans, I felt how difficult it was to change the regular patterns of thoughts, actions, and words. What to say of fighting against negative forces which had aligned to wreak havoc in our lives. These challenges appeared oceanic to be able to overcome.

My grief had taken over me and had made me almost non functional. I had to change but it seemed so difficult and I felt a sense of vulnerability creeping inside my consciousness which left me insecure. Human weakness and frailty were brought to the forefront which inculcated fear in me. I felt as if I was lost and helpless. Did I have to accept everything that life had presented to me? Had I to remain the same as I was a weak and fragile person in front of the outside world and my own limitations? Could I not just redefine myself and fight for the cause which I had just taken as my life's mission.

I sought intervention. I sought help. I longed to be guided to the right path and prayed for enlightenment to the vast ocean and the power that created such a fierce gigantic ocean.

As I was sitting ashore, perplexed, I saw a man comfortably steer a boat. In the boat was a lady and in her arms, was a baby so blissful amidst the strong current of a sea; he appeared happily waving his hands. I assumed they were his family. The child, he was simply enjoying the ocean ride, careless and safe although he was most vulnerable. I found it ironic that he was most vulnerable amongst them to the seas yet he felt safe and happiest. Why? The lights dawned upon me; a child is safest in his mother's arms. He fears no danger in front of him when he takes shelter of his parents. I was sure; his parents would throw away everything and go through any situation just for the comfort, well-being, and safety of the child. It wasn't really about being strong; it was all about having faith in the right shelter.

The lady sat there peacefully too, looking at husband maneuvering through waves of ocean; completely assured that he was in control of both her and her child. With full faith in his capabilities and a natural dependence on him, her face reflected the much sought after peace and security. The husband too seemed unperturbed as he showed his faith and took shelter of a mere boat- a club of planks which had the capability to float, something so wonderful given by nature.

I realized that in reality, my vulnerability was my strength and not a limiting factor. Now I felt powerless but this powerlessness was different, an empowering one. I realized the more vulnerable I felt, the more I would choose dependence, guidance and assistance which would empower me beyond my capabilities. I needed a guiding hand which would sail me through the challenges of a mission I had envisioned to accomplish. I felt having vulnerability was great as long as I had the right guidance and I was taking shelter of it, as long as I accepted the grace and power which was available in this world to those who trod on the righteous path and those who sought after it.

Of course, it was difficult; I had to put aside my ego. I had to put faith; not blind; but at least a calculated one. I had to humbly accept my shortcomings in life. Wouldn't that require me to go beyond my own limitations and leap ahead?

Was I ready for it? All the modern education, technology and media had thumped on me a sense of know-it-all and be-all mindset. Could I overcome it that easily? Time would tell it all. I begged the Almighty to bestow upon me enough power to be able to overcome my barriers and accept His grace coming through people, situations and His own revelations which would be disclosed to me if I remained sincere and persistent on my mission. I felt confident because I was risking for the right cause.

Part I

Double Edged

The television played the news,

"In the Annual General Meeting of Derby Labs, it was announced that the scientists from Derby Labs private limited are working on wartime drugs. They have discovered a drug which will enable soldiers to fight ceaselessly without sleep for 5 consecutive nights without any significant signs of addiction. These drugs will help air force pilots to have a higher level of concentration while having extra-long sorties during wars. They have also discovered antidotes which will be useful in defense against biological warfare, drugs which help soldiers to heal their wounds quick. This is a huge success for the 'Make in India' initiative for our country and this research will attract sales worth millions of dollars. The shares of the company have risen to their all-time high."

Mr. M. Srivastava appeared on the screen, he was the Managing Director of the research wing of the Derby lab firm. Tv anchors aired his interview,

"It is a big success for our company. To our great pride, this is truly an indigenous invention. The Indian army will find this very useful. We will sell this technology to other friendly countries as well. I had dreamt of becoming a successful company director and my dream has finally come true. I sincerely thank all of our crew who worked on this

project tirelessly, especially, Mr. Mandar Sahastrabuddhe and his team. They have headed the research part really well. We also thank all our investors for deeply trusting us for so long."

The Anchor asked Mr. M. Srivastava about the moral integrity of the invention, he explained, "Security forces work in situations that can lead to a lot of mental pressure. In warlike situations, it increases even more. Modern warfare needs soldiers to have an edge over opponents. These drugs will give the necessary boost to our forces when it is most required. Also, now there is an increased danger of biological warfare. Unlike traditional weapons, biological weapons are extremely potent and contagious which can disturb a whole strength of armies at a crucial time. So we should possess antidotes of these biological weapons to tackle any emergency situation"

Ankit's father worked as a freelance business consultant for Derby Labs. I texted him congratulations message for his company's success.

There appeared another news on the TV channel after some time,

"In the last six months, twelve adults were reported to have lost their lives because of a drug overdose. Police are confused about the source of the drugs. Recently it has been found that drugs are being peddled through the dark web, making it almost impossible to find out the source of the drug production or distribution. Police have requested parents to keep watch on their wards to avoid them

falling into this dangerous track"

I felt it quite strange; one news described the glory of drugs, while other news portrayed the gory nature of drugs. In the first case, it was important for the security of the nation, while in other, it was a threat to it.

It seemed everything in the world had to be double-edged. Science, weapons, money, fame, knowledge and so on. You name it and there will be plenty of examples of who use for right purpose and others who use for ulterior motives.

My father would say, "Tanmay, you are what your intentions are, no matter what you do!"

How do I judge my intentions, it was not that easy. The human mind is so complex. One could always find a justification to sanitize something wicked.

Was there any absolute standard as a benchmark to gauge the purity of our intentions against it? Was it fixed like an ISIS dogma or was it fluid and flexible? Did it really matter to worry about it? I hoped to find an answer to this dilemma which popped up every now and then in my life.

Life fizzled out

"Don't distract me, Ankit" Aarya was desperate. She sounded like she would do anything in her power right now to make me sit and talk to her.

But I couldn't, I wouldn't.

"...don't go changing topics. I know what's going on in your mind lately. Don't do anything reckless. Please just talk to me. We'll find some solution. Let me help you."

I could hear her sniveling through the phone. I couldn't help it.

I was trapped. It's frustrating the way I have come to ruin my life. All because I couldn't say no to another dose of drugs. All because I couldn't bring myself turn down another glass of drink. All because I couldn't control my urges.

I ruined everything, my studies, my career, my relationships and so forth. There was a desire burning inside me to put an end to everything – the wanting, the breathing, life itself. Going on had no meaning left for me. However, my sister Aarya understood my situation somehow. She sounded like she would bind me to a chair and make me talk if she could, but she's not here right now. Even though she wanted to help, she couldn't. I didn't need help. I needed an end.

Her sigh echoed deep into my ear, "It's okay if you don't want to talk right now. But just remember that I'm always here whenever you want to talk to me."

"I know," I replied monotonously and then hung up the phone as I didn't want to continue that one particular discussion.

It had been a couple of years or more now that I got dragged into this vicious cycle. I belonged to a well off family. When I was in school, I accompanied my parents to parties that became page-three-talk for the following day. All the affluent flocked together in these places.

Music, food, gossips lied at the heart of these parties. Every party was a sort of pitch among the ones who attended, the ones with the latest trend, the ones with the risqué trend, trends all over – be it fashion, gadgets, people or cars.

Status was the only thing that mattered.

My parents weren't regular drinkers. But that was only at home, in these parties, everyone was expected to down a glass or more. My dad told me how important these parties were in order to develop better future connections.

Downing a glass of whiskey in the party alongside other boys at the party wasn't a big deal when I was a teen; I had seen my parents taking it right from the time I remembered. After all, I was only following suit. Thereafter I began looking forward to these parties. Having friends over when my parents weren't around was another thing I did a lot.

My father after a successful stint as a CFO of a

company became an independent business consultant for various multinational corporations whereas my mother was a fashion designer. Traveling both in and out of India was no big deal for her. She was exceptionally talented at what she did. No wonder she began to receive contracts from high-end multitudes, the Bollywood included.

In my loneliness at home, I kept myself busy, either with games or parties. The only good thing in my life would be that I got whatever I wanted, whenever I wanted it. My father never said no to anything I wished for. After all, money did buy everything, or so he thought. Everyone including my friends thought about how my life was fine, that everything went normally in my house. But of course, it's true that the grass always seems greener on the other side. I felt like a well groomed but a hungry dog.

The only person to whom I felt connected was my sister, Aarya. She was three years older than me and yet, she's the person I felt closer to the most in this broken family of ours. Her innocent smile always decorated her jovial face. We shared all of our secrets. We joked together and studied together. I was athletic, rational and individualist, on the other hand, she was lean, emotional and conforming, but we shared a common bond of love for each other and we loved to fight evil; the love inherited from our maternal grandfather who was an army veteran. But then there came a time when even she left and went away to another city for her junior college. There had never been a time I missed someone so much. I learned what loneliness was when she left.

I then found Tanmay, who became close to my heart. The one person in whom I could confide in without much thought. Even though I was his senior and came from a better background, which led me to never taking his words seriously.

One day, at a party, I heard about "ecstasy" or party pills as they called it, from one of the party goers. Just hearing someone describe cloud nine wasn't enough, I thought. So I sought to try it for myself, the high that they were talking about.

That was the first time I witnessed what drugs could do. Cloud nine was an understatement.

I was taken off the ground.

And then I couldn't let go of it. Couldn't let go of what I'd experienced firsthand which is why I kept having it. Over and over again, in higher doses, as time passed.

I started buying drugs from the dark web and paid with cryptocurrencies. It created the high all to push you off the cliff at some point. Even though somewhere in the back of my mind I realized that things could get out of my hand, I didn't have it in me to give up on the pills that turned me into an entirely different person than what I usually was. I turned into a better person, a person who was reckless without giving much thought to it. The otherwise reserved person that I was, went into hiding once the pill was in me.

I felt powerful; with no pressure in those few

moments. It was a flush of dopamine-bliss and soothe pervaded my being for a flash than a filthy part of it lashed out. The realities crashed into me like a train- flushing out all the peace and whatsoever bliss. There wasn't any coming back from the quicksand of these intoxicants.

And then I began procuring different varieties of drugs to get a better experience. With each trip mind-blowing than the last, my dependence on these drugs grew. And then the urge to have these drugs almost every week too increased.

I became self-centered and cunning. All I cared about was my next dose, no matter what the problem was. When I ran out of money I stole, from home.

I knew I needed help, but it wasn't easy.

Whom would I tell? What would I say? The stigma around addiction and the lash I'd be hit back with made me keep my mouth shut. The shame of being an addict over continuing drugs was too much. My grades kept going south and then there came a time when I realized that my life had become meaningless.

I knew I ruined it all when my lifestyle had pushed my parents and sister into anxiety. Aarya was terrified when I drank heavily and wasted myself on alcohol and came home driving my motorbike, with bruises on my hands and knees from the accidents I used to get into. Another day, I managed to eavesdrop on my mother telling my father how she had nightmares about the things that could happen to me.

My mother was always afraid of my well-being, but it was too late. She couldn't imagine her life without me. Worrying about me and her demanding job took a lot from her. I felt bad, but it really was too late. She wanted me to give up drinking, but unlike how she couldn't imagine her life without me, I, on the other hand, couldn't imagine my life without alcohol.

It was not like I didn't think of giving up on this lifestyle; It was just that it was way too hard. Thinking and actually doing it are things that stand worlds apart.

Addicted; that's what I was. There was no more room for self-control, it was evident that I'd lost my grip on it long back. Actually, I didn't want to give up and die but I felt I was on dead end.

I was helpless.

Trapped

"Tanmay, I want to see you. Can we meet in the afternoon?" Ankit asked me.

I knew things weren't going well in his life. He'd been in a bad shape and I barely saw him in college anymore. I wanted to see him as well.

"Okay Ankit, let's meet up. I'll come over to your place."

When I saw him, it was as if I didn't recognize him. His face had lost all color, his body – weak. With dilated pupils and a face that had seemed to have lost all color, he looked as if he'd been sick all this time. He looked as if he was hiding a grave secret from me.

"Hey, man, what's up? You don't look so good. Is everything okay?" I ask him.

"I'm trapped Tanmay, I don't know what to do anymore," his reply made me nervous. I'd never seen him like this. He was always this stud that everyone looked up to.

"What's wrong? This somber attitude doesn't suit you. Tell me what's going on."

Even though we were standing a few feet apart, he felt disconnected somehow. This silence seemed intriguing, but I feared what he had to say. My earliest memory of him was him being a bright student, a geek even. He talked with such confidence that everyone wanted to listen.

"We must come out of limitations of time, space and thoughts. We cannot illogically subjugate our conscience to dogmas thrust on us by this world. We must experience freedom from all these. We should go beyond the jurisdiction of what is good and bad and we should nurture an attitude of explorer towards life. We should do what our passions direct us to do and care-less about what the world has to say," the speech that Ankit delivered last year had everyone in awe of him.

He and I became friends on the Andheri cricket ground. We represented the same team. We matched in many things like physique, food choices, favorite sports even our political views but he was a hard hitter in the ball game, I always played carefully, keeping my wicket. Since we played together from same team, I started frequenting him and we became very close friends. It was obvious that I'd start getting around with his friends too after then.

We decided to take admission in the same college. Slowly, his habits started rubbing off on me. I might have been a little apprehensive about his habits in the beginning but soon I became one of his accomplices.

Coming out of the flashback, I couldn't believe my eyes that Ankit was in front of me, looking lost, almost as if he'd left his self somewhere else.

His face broke something in me and I told him, "If it's bothering you so much, why don't you stop taking drugs?"

"I tried. But nothing seems to work. I have been trying for a while now, but every time I resolve to give up, I find myself sinking in deeper than I was before. My body doesn't feel like my own if I don't take it. Relentless shivering and then the exasperation have no end. All I can focus is on my next dose because I don't want to keep feeling this way. Help me, Tanmay."

"How can I possibly help you with this?" I asked him,

"Do you remember the first time you took me with you to one of your parties? How you had me cornered with all of your friends? You asked me to give it a try and then decide if I wanted to go on doing it.

I had an inferiority complex. Most of our other friends were from upper-class families. Branded things, partying on the weekends, foreign vacations, premium sports club memberships, latest gadgets, and vehicles etc. were common among them. I knew I stood nowhere near all the other guys. Which was why I wished to crack the IIT examination and join a prestigious institute but I failed. My hopes were shattered. I could never be a part of the society Ankit belonged to. I lied and imitated but it wouldn't work for long, I knew. So when I was given the choice to go ahead and try alcohol for the first time in my life, I didn't hesitate much. I loosened my morals a bit because I refused to be seen as the uptight timid guy who was afraid of embracing something new. Later I began smoking and then, it became another pattern for me. It was one of my biggest regrets. After I started doing the things that they all did just so I could kind of fit among them.

Shaking off the memories, I asked, "How can I help you now? When you're the one who got me in the quicksand with you anyway?"

I could see the guilt making way from his eyes to his lips, "Yes, It was my mistake, I dragged you in all of this but now I realize it's definitely life jeopardizing. I have started to realize that even I was forced to make this choice by propaganda-Media propaganda and even anti-national elements."

"I understand when you say about media. Companies spend a huge amount of money on the promotion of these intoxicating substances. The actors, sport-stars, business tycoons brandish these intoxicants as if it is a non-detachable part of their regale personality and people follow them blindly. But how are anti-national elements involved in this?"

Ankit sighed and replied, "Because there is big money in this. Do you know the drug cartels of Mexico are one of the biggest billionaires in the world? They'll commit the worst crimes just to smuggle these products all over the world. And their power is boundless because of their hard hold over the economy, politics, technology, corporations, media etc. El Chapo the biggest drug lord of all time from Mexico fled most tight security jail twice before he was caught again just recently. Similar cartels are existing across the border of India, funding terror and weakening the youth of this blessed country. I feel so miserable that I got myself caught in their net."

Ankit continued, "First we need to reform ourselves. And spread awareness about this to all the people around us. And we must act against the people who are engaged in these activities, neutralizing their network and efforts. It won't be easy because the whole system is corrupt. If we do something that garners the attention of the wrong crowd, we may get into a problem. But thanks to social media, we have got the power of the common masses. If we gather enough evidence and share across with people, we can get them to support us and then nobody can do anything to us"

"It seems that you are on some kind of mission," listening to him in awe.

Ankit chuckled, "Mission impossible, I am far too bound by these substances that I feel helpless but I want to do something for this cause before something happens to me! There is a deep racket working and scheming to bring drugs in this country and spread it. It is being operated by the foreign spy agency"

I was shaken with this revelation as I replied, "What did you say? How do you know about it?"

"Yesterday, the boy that supplies me my share of the drug revealed everything to me in a stupor.

He overheard this fact in his office. There is a conspiracy to spoil our Indian youth. There is a whole racket operating to peddle drugs and I heard the money is being used for funding terror operations."

I replied, "This is a matter of deep concern, are you going to report it to the police?"

"Not for now, it is too early. Also, the boy pleaded me to not to reveal this information to anyone because his whole life is supported by that income and if it stops then it will be disastrous. I will myself do some investigation in this matter and disclose this to appropriate people who can handle it."

"Ankit, please be careful, this is a serious matter and these people appear to be very sly."

I'll always miss you

Around 4 in the evening, my phone rang. The voice on the other end was sobbing and I couldn't make out who it was. The next words that came out of the phone had my breath hitched and then my life was never to be the same again.

"Our Ankit is no more. He's gone, Tanmay, he's left us."

I thought that if this was what pain felt like, I didn't want to feel it anymore. I couldn't move for a while. I wanted to rewind the past three minutes, so as to never have heard those words.

At some point, the cell phone slipped out of my hand and hit the floor with a dull thud. I fell down right beside my phone- gravity far too heavy for my knees to keep me standing anymore. It felt as if time had stopped then and there. My stomach dropped as I replayed the message in my mind over and over again.

Ankit was dead. He was gone. My friend was no more.

I grabbed my bike keys and drove off to Ankit's house only to see a bunch of people mostly his relatives, all dressed in white. Mourning his death.

They were talking about how Ankit had taken his own life. I knew this wasn't possible. Even after everything that he'd been going through, I knew that he wasn't one to give up easily. I wanted to scream and tell everyone that Ankit hadn't committed suicide, but I couldn't.

The scene was horrific. I had never in my life imagined such a scene, at least not having Ankit in it. I still kept asking myself, why? Why would he take his own life? His mother had her eyes all swollen and couldn't stop crying. His sister, Aarya, was consoling her mother still trying to contain her grief. His father had a blank expression while sitting on the white rug, tears threatening to pull him apart.

I walked over towards his mother to give say something that would help but I couldn't utter a single word. All she did was sob; all I did was stand there - helpless.

I went ahead and asked his father.

His father said, "He was found dead in his room at home. His mother went to see him and found him lying on the bed all pale... His body was cold and muscles were tightened. He did not wake up after being repeatedly called and nudged. I tested his pulse and breathing, it had stopped. I could feel it in my bones, he wasn't there anymore. But his mother kept on shaking him trying to wake him up as if he was only asleep and had to be woken, she could not digest the fact that her child was no more. Yet we called the doctors for a final declaration, they declared him dead. His body was sent for post-mortem. The cause ascertained for his death was a drug overdose. He had killed himself with a drug overdose."

"When did this happen?"

"Till late in the morning he did not come out of his room so around noon, his mother went to his room and found him lying there motionless. He might have taken the drugs yesterday night. It is so unfortunate that nobody was present at home at that time. We had gone to a party organized by Mr. M. Srivastava for our recent success at Derby Labs. I was obliged to go as I work for them. Mr. Srivastava was visibly very sick and Mr. Mandar had to drop him to hospital in middle because of his very bad health but he had made sure, the guests would be thoroughly entertained, we got caught up in the show. We could have left in between but we remained stuck up there. The party went till late in the night and this is what we see today. We are so unfortunate."

I went along with them to the crematorium for a final goodbye. His father lit the pyre. He had a fire in his hands and water in his eyes, the earthly remains of the body of his son returning to the original chunk of earth. Ether was still echoing the heartrending cries of his mother and sister, the body was lit and soon air carried the smoke, not as pleasant as liked by junkies.

There were whispers during his cremation about his possible reason for death. Police sealed the crime scene and collected evidence. His addiction to drugs and the threats of suicide he gave to his family had weakened the case. The Police had already categorized this case under a 'suicide category' and if no leads were found soon, the investigation file would be closed and dumped in the closet which had thousands of other closed files. There were no complaints from his family for further investigation.

Personally, I was confused. Ankit had been talking of taking his own life but at the same time he had discussed his plans related to a mission about exposing something and he was not the kind of person who would give up a mission before fruition. I made a plan to personally investigate the matter. After all, he was like a brother to me and now to imagine my life without Ankit? How could I possibly live like that? After his departure, all I felt was a huge void, a gaping hole that only Ankit could fill up.

My heart became heavy with sadness. I knew that in such a situation there was only one haven for me. I went to the nearest bar and after an hour or three; my other friends pulled me out of there. The reality was painful and I wanted to forget it. I went to my room and dozed off, not wishing to wake up the next morning either. The next day, when I was finally awake, I found myself sinking in grief again.

It was too difficult to forget him. I spent some time on the bed just rolling over from side to side. I got up, went out and drank again. It became a cycle for me, for a number of days. My parents knew that I was in mourning but they were confused with my new behavior. I just told them to give me some space and everything would be back to normal in a few days.

Life's Mission

I opened my closet and from the corner, I took out an old dusty box. It contained our old family pictures. Our happy family. Where I was happy with my brother, Ankit, and both my parents.

We had all fond memories stored in those pages of the album. Tears fell in torrents on the photos as I longed for my brother to come back to me. I went out of the city for my junior college studies. Regardless, we would talk every single day for a solid one hour. Our bond was strong. He was my little brother after all. I was the one who took care of him, apart from my mother. He was like a child to me.

I used to express myself but he kept everything inside, well cooped up. He would not easily talk about his feelings. I knew the art of slowly helping him cope with those emotions. But how long was I going to support him? As the years passed and responsibilities increased; it became difficult to connect with each other. His addiction progressed so fast and we realized it only when it was too late. I was overcome with depression. We were all silently suffering then. And after his death, the suffering became unbearable.

I still felt if I had taken proper measures, I could have done something to save him from being an addict. It's difficult to say what would have made him not take to those drugs but we all blame ourselves for the ill fortune which fell upon us.

However, weeks passed by and I still couldn't let go of the pain and suffering. After meeting Tanmay, I got to know that Ankit was preparing for uncovering of a drugs module which operated on the dictates of the foreign elements. I felt proud that he had started thinking beyond himself and he was wishing to volunteer for such a risky but honorable cause. I personally had developed hatred against the drugs and the powers behind this menace which had created varieties of problems in our family. I felt inspired by mission my brother was going to undertake and in his absence I felt compelled to carry on what he had decided to do but at the same time being a woman and kind of timid personality, I was not sure whether I would be able do that. I had to decide whether I should investigate Ankit's death which I suspected as a murder and carry on the mission he had planned or I should just be peacefully settled in my own life.

I went to the seaside for spending some time along with my mother. The grandeur and the depth of the sea always helped me go deeper and find out even bigger arrangements behind life-events. It was something like self-counseling in the presence of the big sea. My own reflective, meditative part gained upper-hand over my lower self. Solutions emerged in my heart and I felt nourished. With the same desire to grip on these negative layers of emotions, I planned to go ashore.

While having a walk on the ocean shore I saw a few children making sand forts. Each one had his own fort and it appeared that they were competing whose fort would be better. After walking a few more steps, I saw a sand sculpture illustrating and condemning the malpractice of women feticide while visitors flocked around discussing the sculpture.

A realization dawned on me. The fort and sculpture both were made of sand and after a while, both would be washed away. But forts created by children attracted competition and sculptures attracted admiration. If I would work for my own self then I would be like any other person in the race of life but if I were to give my life for a higher cause, then it would make my life meaningful even for others.

The mission was clear, I had to deal with the drug menace which had taken Ankit's life and I had to find out what caused the death of Ankit. Ankit's death was the turning point in my life.

I was also concerned about Tanmay. He was a close friend of Ankit and had become an integral part of our family too. His sudden death had caused him to go numb. He was so highly disturbed that he couldn't sleep peacefully anymore. He had taken shelter of the same despicable tools, mainly alcohol. I knew I had to do something for him as well. I wasn't going to sit back again and watch him go down the same path as my Ankit.

Of course, I had my own apprehensions. Who

would hear me? What difference would it make to the world? As a young lady, will I be able to do it? The task would not be easy. By nature, I was a timid and reserved girl who was happy in the boundary walls of family. It had already taken the life of Ankit; probably I might face lethal threats, was I ready for it?

The words of Martin Luther King, Jr. from our literature course inspired me, 'Our lives begin to end the day we become silent about things that matter'. I couldn't just sit silent.

The vast sea made me realize my insignificance. And a boat riding on the ocean with a happy family made me realize that if I took shelter of the higher arrangement then I could cross this sea of my weakness and frailties. My vulnerability would prove my strength.

I went to Tanmay's home and convinced his parents to send him to a rehab center for some time. Convincing Tanmay, on the other hand, was not an easy task. I called him to my home to discuss his situation.

"Aarya, what's the matter, you called me in such haste?" Tanmay appeared puzzled. His unkempt clothes and disheveled hair bespoke his agonizing situation.

"I know your condition after Ankit's death. You have been unable to control your pain and you are drinking almost every day, it's bad."

"Nothing like that, I am in control of things. Yeah it is true that his death has hurt me and I am finding shelter in wine but things are in control"

"Do not give prevarications, your mom informed me. You are totally out of order and in complete disarray. If you were in control, it wouldn't need you to drink every single day. Somebody told me, you created ruckus at the bar couple of days ago. I know everything. In my opinion, you should seriously consider moving to a rehabilitation center. You are too like my brother, I do not want to lose you after Ankit." I said conclusively in a serious tone. "Look in my eyes and tell me- are you happy with the way you are going ahead?"

"No. Even I want to give up this. But, it is too much to move to a rehabilitation center. What people will think? I will appear like a loser. One who had to admit the defeat. It will prove, I couldn't control myself. Some people had already warned me to stop boozing. Seeing me in rehabilitation center, I will be proved foolish in front of them."

"Why do you care about what people will say? Did you care about the people when you fuddle? There will be always some people who will like what you do and some other people who will criticize for your actions. But if you go to a center now, you will be able to gain back control of your life and heal yourself."

"Ok. I accept. I will move there. But only for a month!"

Part II

Sharanam

We had heard of the successful rehabilitation center 'Sharanam.' After checking with a few people, we decided to admit Tanmay there. There was a smaller gate in the big iron gate, which opened to allow us inside. The entry was restricted and the admitted addict could go out only after a month. I saw some people smoking just before entering the gate- hopefully their last cigarette. Inside it had exquisite interiors which were pleasing to the mind. It was congested that day as it was the admission day at the rehabilitation center. Addicts with their guardians were waiting in the lounge filling forms for information to be processed and waiting for further confirmation of their approval for enrollment in the center. The director Mr. Vikas Chafekar then welcomed us very warmly.

After meeting Mr. Vikas, we decided to meet the counselor, Mr. Rupesh Gaikwad in his cabin as there was plenty of time before we were to be called for our turn. As we entered, there sat a brawny man in his thirties, with a fair complexion. He wore a cotton white shirt and dark blue trousers. He was busy quickly fixing various tasks which were interrupted by frequent calls.

I proceeded to explain our case, "Sir, we are yet not able to accept the trauma which has been caused by the death of my brother who was dear friend of Tanmay sitting beside me. I am internally suffering but he has resorted to alcohol to drown his pain in it but the pain manages to resurface every time. How do we handle this situation?"

He replied, "Handling emotions is important for our sound health. Specifically, people dislike negative emotions like fear, disgust, pain, misery, grief, anger, remorse, etc."

I said, "You are right, but how do we get on with our lives when we come across such feelings? It's so frightening to accept the situations which cause such emotions. Even in a dream, I wouldn't like to encounter those."

He said, "Nobody will, but we have to realize our vulnerability as we are tiny beings in this enormous universe and we do not own enough powers to have full control of our lives. Life may throw us in numerous difficult situations. If we continue to hold on to our current pleasant state and deny our vulnerability; then we are bound to suffer when things go wrong."

Hearing this, I replied, "I pondered over this too- my reflection was that once I accepted my vulnerability and opened myself for guidance and grace, I felt empowered."

"We have to embrace the uncertainty. We need to understand that we have little control over things befalling upon us and people around. We have to accept these displeasing emotions also when they come in on our path. We need to deal with our problems rather than denying them. But if we choose to deny our pain or grief, it simply doesn't disappear, it instead gets suppressed, and we experience them anyway in form of outbursts. We have to be grateful for even a pain which we feel because it's a sign of life we are allowed to live."

"Could you care to explain more about this?"

"If you are always remorseful about what has happened in your life and don't accept it, then your grief has no way out and you will feel depressed. But if you accept your grief no matter how difficult it is for you, you will overcome this emotion. Similarly, if you are too fearful about difficult situations in life, then it is a sign that you are too attached to your sense of security which alarms you."

I said, "You are indeed insightful in the science of feelings and emotions! To accept these negative emotions is difficult but I understand now that I have to accept it. Can you please guide more about how to approach such feelings?"

Gaikwad replied, "These feelings are responses to situations. Your conscience does not distinguish between what is real or unreal, it responds with emotions. The simple key is not to block but feel those emotions and think or judge less about them. Even it is better to not do anything during outbursts of emotion. In this process, you become more aware of yourself and your core values. You can work on your core values by aligning them to absolute values which you can learn from the life of great souls. Even the oriental wisdom teaches the art of mindfulness. It distinguishes between seer and seen, the experience and the knower of experience. So according to this, we always have the chance to improve ourselves."

"We also hope that staying at this place under your guidance and observation will definitely help Tanmay," I added with a smile full of hope.

"We sympathize over what has happened to you and your family and we are with you to help you cross this over," he said. Gaikwad then further elaborated, "Here, you will definitely find a support system which will help Tanmay to come out of this trauma and addiction. However, he has to take the final call of internalizing lessons which are learned here into his life. He has to accept that he is in trouble and he needs this program. Addiction not only physically affects a person but also changes their thinking and behavioral pattern. They learn negative patterns of dealing with money, relationship, time which in turn affects the family, job, education, career etc. The de-addiction center helps such an addict to pull through and at the same time heals all the other aspects of life which are affected."

"What is the general program which is followed here?" I inquired curiously.

He answered, "We wake up early in the morning, and we have Yoga (Pranayama) sessions, morning prayers, breakfast, and the day followed by internal services. We have group sessions about various topics related to addiction. At our rehabilitation center, various services are managed by the patients themselves. Finally, in the evening, we gather again for exercises and prayers which are followed by a video film. All our programs are important, specifically the group sessions where people share their experiences while the listeners relate to it and find an emotional connection among them which helps them gain an enormous amount of strength to give up addiction and heal what is damaged. We also make our patients go through certain steps of recovery which help them to overcome their addiction."

"Sir, we are keeping Tanmay under your vigilance. He was the best friend of my younger brother so he means more than a friend to me- he's like a brother. I am answerable to his parents too. Please do take care of him," I implored Gaikwad.

12 Steps of Escape

"Tanmay, this is the first time that I have seen you so happy here!" said Larry.

I was pleased to know somebody identified my feelings. "It is the first time that the day has been so smooth".

Initially, the days were immensely tough- I was grappling with withdrawal symptoms where I would feel sick, nauseated and experience insomnia. Gradually they ebbed away. I really missed home. I'd say I was more homesick than physical sick. Staying with a bunch of people who had similar addictions to different substances was indeed strange for me. Although the food was sumptuous, it wasn't the same as home-cooked meals. Over a few days, I became good friends with Larry from Goa who was a volunteer here for helping addicts.

"Larry, can you please tell me about your journey towards de-addiction?" I asked him one day.

He replied, "I used to drink a lot. After my university graduation, my long term relationship ended badly. I did not handle that part of life well and I was in dire need of emotional support, but couldn't have it then. I joined a hospitality department in one of the hotels where alcohol and drugs were very common and easily available. I will tell you an interesting quote by Mr. Alec Matta to explain my falling into drugs, 'Making the wrong decision starts when making the right decision would have been easy but we didn't think it as important as it were.' Somehow I lost control of my life. I lost my clear ability of clear and independent thought. One day I had a harrowing experience. I woke up with black eyes and only patchy memories about the previous night. I was alarmed. I then realized it was getting too late but not too late to right all my wrongs. Finally, I decided to get in touch with a support group for cocaine addicts."

He further narrated, "Initially I was not serious about this, and I thought it would be a funny, entertaining and really good story to tell at the pub, but when I enquired about it I actually found a group of people who knew how I felt before I even said anything out loud. They listened to me without judgment. I was accepted when I was completely broken. I found a connection. Moreover, the twelve steps taught here is what keeps me sober since the time I have stopped taking alcohol."

"What is this twelve steps program? And what are those steps? Could you please give a walk-through?" I requested him to explain to me the twelve steps that helped him back to sobriety.

"Twelve-step methods have been adapted to address a wide range of alcoholism, substance abuse and dependency problems. It currently has millions of followers across the world now and it has helped many people to give up their addiction not only alcohol and drugs but also internet, gaming, gambling, food, porn, etc.

I will explain one by one each step to you.

The first step: *We admit that we are powerless over our addiction, that our lives have become unmanageable.* This is the most difficult thing for an addict- to accept one's own helpless state and to realize that he is not in control of himself. Generally, we tend to think that we can control ourselves or we can manage our lives when we want, the way we want, but an addict acknowledges his helplessness against addiction. They make innumerable promises to not to fall into it again but when they fail to keep the promise; they lose all hope."

"Did you ever feel it going beyond your control?"

"Even in my skewed perception at the peak of my addiction, I could see that my life was unmanageable. I got flashes in front of my eyes, numbness in my fingers and toes and even nosebleeds. As a twenty-three-year-old with extreme memory loss, I didn't bathe regularly nor did I open my emails. I became detached and developed a really unattractive facial twitch that would set off at the most inconvenient moments. It had gone beyond my power. All in all, I was a complete mess. And still, I could not give up the addiction. It kept me running.

And in such a case, one cannot depend upon one's own mental and intellectual abilities for right guidance. Even addictions like porn, gambling, TV, eating are subtle and they gradually thwart our ability to think whether they are any good for us. So one's own intellectual and mental abilities can cheat oneself at any given moment. We need to find out somebody who can help us as given in the step two and three."

Even I had lost my control over alcohol. Initially, I thought it would give me the power to deal with painful things in my life but I had ended up with more problems than solutions. I really got interested so I requested him, "Please continue."

"Second and third step: We came to believe that a power greater than us could restore us to sanity. And made a decision to turn our will and our lives over to the care of God as we understood Him.

This was incredibly liberating for me. I always felt like I was a kind of a supreme ruler where my decisions dictated everything and everyone in my life, only to realize that actually, I'm not that supreme. I don't have that kind of power which meant that I could make the wrong decisions and give myself the grace to learn from them. I needed help. It is important to feel need of a help when we want to get out of an addiction. I'm a Christian and so, I found that higher power or God in church. But for other people, it is their own faith or even simple acknowledgment that a group of people gathered together for a common purpose is more powerful than one person on his own.

In this program, the first thing we do is stop using drugs. At this point, we begin to feel the pain of living without drugs. The pain that we feel forces us to seek a power greater than ourselves which helps overcome our obsession. We have to find who that higher power is for us. We keep faith in the sanity of the higher power over our own and wholeheartedly accept their suggestions and apply them in our life. We have misused our independence and ended up abusing our body, and therefore, we depend on a higher power to help us to be better. We are ready for a change in our current pattern of thinking, feeling or willing. We should find and study about people who have changed their lives substantially by accepting the help from a power beyond them, people who live by the spiritual principles in their lives. It will give us faith that it works."

I pointed out, "This is quite similar to what I heard from my granny about Arjun who surrendered in the sacred book of Gita! Although Arjun was a great warrior and learned scholar, He lost his discrimination in the battlefield, he told Krishna who was guiding him as a Guru that he could not understand what was right or wrong and was thoroughly confused, so Arjun accepted him as teacher and guide. Submitting himself completely under his care, he got the perfect guidance, as we see in the book."

Smiling with his fingers steepled, "Similarly we

have to submit ourselves to a power greater than us. We have applied our faith on the material things like phone, sex, drugs etc. to find satisfaction, that same faith we need to redirect to a power beyond ourselves, the power of spirituality to get the direction. The misdirected faith has caused chaos, we have to find person and systems where we can redirect our love and find real relief and satisfaction. Once we have chosen our guide, we have to first come to terms with our wrongs in step four and five. Unless we accept our wrongs, the guide cannot help us, to put it in other words, we would not seek any change unless we accept our wrongs. This forms the base for the next steps. Are you eager to go ahead?"

I smilingly approved. I was more than excited to know further.

"Steps four and five: We searched for a tireless and fearless moral inventory of ourselves and we admitted to God, to ourselves, and to another human being the exact nature of our wrongs.

In this step, we begin to get in touch with ourselves. We write about our liabilities, the things, and feelings which put us down such as the mistakes we have committed, the guilt and shame we feel, any remorse or self-pity we have, something which has caused us resentment or anger, all our anxieties, and fears, etc. We write about the things that bother us here and now.

We have a tendency to think negatively, so putting it on paper gives us a chance to look more positively at what is happening around us and then processing our thoughts thus giving insight to our own inner mind. We also write about our past mistakes. An addict sees himself as a person with very fewer flaws or rather almost perfect. So much of their time and energy is spent to perfect that image standing in front of the world that they are ignorant to the "person" inside. We thought we'd keep such an image in the forefront and would be accepted. We feared to let go of our image as we feared the world's judgment. We thought that this would fool the world and we'd be accepted but did you care to notice how much it had disrupted us from the inside? Most often we don't. Our self-esteem comes in the way. The need for being accepted is all-consuming and thus we deny our true selves.

These masks need to fall off. We share our inventory as it is written, specifying everything and if possible on a deeper note. We continue to approach this step with honesty and thoroughness until we finish. It is a great relief to get rid of all our past baggage. The lighter the baggage, the easier and more comfortable is the journey. We slowly begin to apply the given solutions and correct our mistakes. So I will request you to personally take time and write down your own inventory of assets and liabilities"

I felt anxious with the thought of exposing all my past deeds in front of others. I hesitated, "But it is so tough to dig up a pile of all your mistakes and sharing all our weaknesses with another person."

He checked his watch as the bell for the common exercise would soon ring but seeing me so eager; he decided to extend.

"Some people don't even get to the end of the 12 steps because they look at it as a much tougher way than going back to drugs. But it has to be done and we have to find one person who will not judge us but empathetically accept us. I sorted it out by writing four lists- I wrote a list of everything I was afraid of, every time I'd ever hurt another person in my life, every sexual encounter I'd ever had and every resentment I was carrying. When I saw all my mistakes jotted down on paper, I couldn't believe how angry and guilty I was. It was hard to fathom the fact that I had engaged in such moral wrongdoings, I felt like I was drowning in a pool of guilt and burdened with such mistakes. It was overwhelming. I remembered a quote just then- "To forgive is to set a prisoner free and discover that the prisoner was you" by Lewis B. Smedes. Well, I learned to forgive myself; I am free from such allegations! Sharing such burdens out loud to someone willing to hear it and who will console you and actually understand you the way you are, makes you realize the fact that you aren't as bad as you thought.

When that happens, something changes inside you. You feel lighter and a spark of hope ignites inside and you move on with a brighter outlook for the future. Just like a detox cleanses your body out of toxins; it frees you from all the burdens you have embedded in yourself. We have to find a person whom we can trust to share everything about our lives and who is only interested in helping us out, this is very essential. This step also helps us to get out of our loneliness. Most of the addicts suffer from loneliness which propels them further into addiction. Step five helps to solve this problem. After this, in order to remain on the right path always; we have to accept and apply the teachings of the guide as given in steps six and seven"

The bell had already rung, but the discussion was getting so interesting that I just requested him to continue for some more time.

"Steps six and seven: We were entirely ready to have God remove all these defects of character. And we humbly asked Him to remove our shortcomings.

It is our human nature to commit various mistakes. But by sharing those mistakes and undertaking sincere guidance to overcome them, we come out stronger than we were before and with a firm personality."

I felt restless again thinking of a person directing me about my own habits, the amount of control of my life I would give to others, the change I would have to undergo and what my friends would think of me… "I find some distorted security in familiar pain. How do I become one hundred percent ready to let it go?"

He said, "We have to accept that our defects drain away all our precious energy. We can think about how the defects listed in the earlier step are going to harm us in the longer run. What is most important in our life which at stake because of our wrong habits? Our job, our relationships, our family...

This step also paves way for humility which is important to accept our faults. In order to realize that we couldn't let it go on our own and we can't do it now; we need help. These faults have already affected us and that's why we are here. So a keen desire to get rid of all of this will help us follow these steps. Only by accepting the suggestions and corrections by others, can we then grow and change every single day."

He paused to recollect his thoughts, "When I wrote down all my suppressed feelings, I discovered times when I had gone wrong and acted out in a selfish manner. I prioritized the drinking and drugs above all my friends and family. I noticed that I had not attended my dearest friend's father's funeral and failed to console him when he needed me because I was too busy getting drunk and high. When I dug even deeper, it became apparent that there was a common denominator underneath all those defects and that was fear. I was making all my decisions based on the fear of being unpopular, fear of being disliked and being rejected- fear of everything. But now I understand that and by gradually accepting the fear, I can be what I actually am and give people a chance to see that. Even I am able to now deal with it by taking solutions to come out of that fear mentality.

As we have reformed on the personal level, we have to also reform on the relationship and social level, which is part of steps eight and *nine.*"

Sighing, he continued, *"Steps eight and nine: We made a list of all persons we had harmed and strived to make amends with them all. And we made direct amends with them wherever possible, except when doing so would injure them or others."*

I wondered if he memorized all this by heart.

He said, "Writing those lists can seem to be hard, but, it is not so, rather it's a reinvigorating process. At the top of my list were the people I had let down- my family and friends. For instance, the friend whose father's funeral I failed to attend," he sighed, his eyes full of remorse.

"You don't go through addiction without hurting the ones who love you the most. When I was in deep addiction, I would sometimes stay with my sister. She'd come up to my room to call me for breakfast and often I wouldn't be there as I'd be out drinking, taking drugs or partying with complete strangers. Finally a year later, when I became sober, I moved in with her. For the first few days, she would come up at 5 am and push the door open just to check if I was still in bed. Such was her fear that I might have relapsed and gone out on a bender. It's that kind of fear, anxiety, and pain that we have to make amends for. So that's what I did! Some people accepted my apologies and were so overwhelmingly gracious that I became exceedingly overwhelmed. It was life-altering. Yet, there were others who didn't reply at all and some just weren't ready to hear from me and that's fine. It was not about the reactions; it was the fact that I was doing right by my part that mattered most. I had the humility to make those amends which meant that I was becoming the kind of person that I wanted to be."

Motivated, I gestured towards him, "You tell me, how long does it take to do all these steps?"

"That is a good question and coincidentally the next steps talk about the same."

He paused, reached for a glass of water and continued,

"Step ten and eleven: *Continued to take personal inventory and when we were wrong promptly admitted it. Sought through prayer and meditation to improve our conscious contact with God as we understood Him, praying only for knowledge of His will for us and the power to carry that out.*

So that every day, we will look at what we've done that day and then make amends for whatever we did wrong which is a lot easier than doing it years later! Most importantly, we made time for ourselves- Pray, Meditate, Reflect.

"And the last step?" I prodded him.

"It is said, the attack is the best defense. We help others on the path of de-addiction which is step twelve- the last of all the steps. Step twelve: *Having had a spiritual awakening as a result of these steps; we then carry this message to other recovering addicts to practice these principles in all our affairs.*

So the spiritual awakening they're talking here

is about anyone who's worked through these twelve steps and they will surely tell you that it is quite powerful and effective. One simply can't explain the way it changes lives without having experienced it. Today, I aspire to share the same with the people who come here for treatment," he smiled widely.

"In my time here right from treatment to becoming a volunteer; I have seen many addicts step in the center with the same urges for drugs or alcohol that I too had, the same pain that I too suffered. I saw them struggle here with all their will to conquer their urges and finally pull through. Some have even taken up volunteering like me and help other people curb their addiction."

By the time he finished his whole recovery and twelve steps program; my respect for him had increased tenfold with every word he spoke. Truly, he had fought a battle both- inside and outside. He was a living example to all other addicts about overcoming a pitiful situation and becoming a social worker. "Wow! You had a great transformation journey and I am grateful for your sharing it with me so openly. Do you feel these steps will also be beneficial to someone who is not an addict?"

He laughed, "One doesn't need to hit rock bottom or get a black eye to start incorporating this kind of principles in one's life. You can admit that you're not completely in control- that you're not the higher power. You can always take stock of where life has brought you and talk to somebody about it honestly. You can identify character defects and then work on them. You can apologize when you've wronged someone and even spare some time to pray, meditate every day. Try to go out there and help other people and you will find yourself happier and more satisfied in life. One may be struggling with any kind of addiction, whether it be booze, drugs or gambling, sex or porn, shopping, and even food! But then you have to do something about it. One can't just do it regularly and feel guilty and miserable. It is okay if one has not been able to sort this out on their own; I couldn't either! Almost no one actually is able to make it on their own. We all need help to do so."

I then remembered a book about the effects of alcohol and how to overcome it. However, today, having a person in front of me who not only fought battles to overcome the addiction but also transformed himself into a social servant dedicated to helping others really inspired me. I felt as if I myself had transformed into a more confident and knowledgeable person. By joining this rehab center, I found not only the will and strength to overcome addiction but also a lifetime friend who'd support me emotionally and keep me off drugs for good.

He was murdered

I went to Dr. Rishabh's office in the city to discuss the forensic reports of Ankit's autopsy. He was a well-known medico-legal advisor in the city. His office was painted in vibrant light green while the large Madhuban style painting in the waiting lounge caught everyone's attention. There were few people waiting there. An ornate flower pot sat on the table decorated with various beautiful flowers and a mild intoxicating fragrance came from the golden Kadamba flowers which saturated the room. The interior speakers played soft, melodious instrumental flute music. Astonishingly, even being in the city, the mooing cows were audible through the windows. Mrs. Kalindi Giriraj, the receptionist across the table took my details. Although I was tense, I felt inexplicably happy standing in the room. After a while, she suddenly announced, "Ms. Aarya, you can meet the doctor inside his cabin."

Breaking out of my reverie, I hurriedly collected Ankit's autopsy reports. It was quite technical and it took more than a month to obtain a detailed report after his death. I reached the cabin of Dr. Rishabh Kumar Singh and saw a glass door with his credentials- M.D. FMT. , L.L.B. Medico Legal advisor. He was also a elder family friend of mine. Greeting him, I sat opposite him on a scratchy chair while he examined the reports. Many officers had suspected that he committed suicide like in other overdose cases.

"Sir, before we get into the report, I have some questions regarding addiction; I wish to clarify from you."

He nodded.

I asked, "I always get confused about all these biology terms dopamine, brain circuitry, etc. Can you please explain what makes a drug so addictive that person just can't stop himself taking it, although it being fatal. It just like foolish moths enter the fire"

He explained, "Our brain is wired to increase the odds that we will repeat a pleasurable activity and the neurotransmitter dopamine is central to this. Whenever there is a healthy, pleasurable experience, a burst of dopamine signals that something important is happening that needs to be remembered. This dopamine signal causes changes in neural connectivity that make it easier to repeat the activity again and again without thinking about it, leading to the formation of habits.

Just as drugs produce intense euphoria; they also produce larger surges of dopamine, thus powerfully reinforcing the connection between the drug consumption and the resulting pleasure. These surges of dopamine 'teach' the brain to seek drugs at the expense of other, healthier goals and activities. Over a period of time, we become habituated to the drug and we need higher doses of dopamine to get the same pleasure. In that case, one needs to increase the drug quantity."

"Doctor, what are the consequences one may face because of addiction? And how one can come out of it?"

"These drugs make changes in our brain pattern, and the person becomes psychologically, physically dependent. A person who indulges in substance abuse loses his focus- he can't recollect or grasp things as quickly as others; he becomes easily irritable and disturbed. In certain serious cases, the person starts experiencing hallucinations. But still, he finds difficult to give up an addiction. If a person refrains from drugs this can be reversed. However, the best time to turn away from drugs is quitting before you even begin."

"Sir, the police at prima facie indicated that it was a suicide. How do the drugs influence suicidal thoughts? How do these drugs work that one moment they put you in intense euphoria and in another moment they depress you completely that you feel suicidal?"

The doctor replied, "The drugs create an inferiority complex in the heart of the addict as he becomes more and more dependent on drugs. Unless he accepts external help, he will fail to come out of it on his own. The economic, social, moral and spiritual harm created by addiction along with the inability to give it up becomes a causal factor for addicts to consider suicide.

Drugs and alcohol can also influence a person

who is already suicidal, making him more impulsive and likely to act upon his urges than if he were sober. Use of drugs and alcohol can contribute to the other reasons people commit suicide, such as the loss of jobs and relationships. Additionally, the rates of substance and alcohol abuse are higher among people with depression and other psychological disorders. Put all these together and the risks increase. So we request people to not take intoxicants or give away if they already use."

"Ok doctor. Thank you for carefully explaining", I said, "Can you please observe the reports and let us know if that was a suicide or homicide? Because I personally feel that it was not a suicide."

Dr. Rishabh glanced closely at the report for some time, his eyes poring over each word carefully. I was beginning to wonder if something was amiss when he exclaimed, "Since drugs are taken in the right arm and he was himself a right-handed person, so there is a possibility that someone else has injected him drugs! The tissue samples also indicated that he had a fresh dosage in that arm as compared to the left arm. His left arm is full of track marks indicating his regular way of injecting drugs but the right arm has only one such mark- this is also a sign that someone else might have injected him with the drugs."

Dr. Rishabh also analyzed crime report, he said, "Moreover, the glass collected from the crime scene was especially clean when compared other dusty glasses. It seems that the other person who was present there tried to wash the glass of alcohol so nobody would be suspicious before he went outside. The forensic analysis of that glass also shows that fragments of fingerprints and lip marks which do not match Ankit's prints; which means there was another person present there along with Ankit."

A dreaded feeling settled in the pit of my stomach. "Sir what does this clearly indicate? Did somebody kill him?"

"Collective evidence suggests the possibility of a homicide."

As I came out of the clinic I was becoming more certain about my suspicion that it was a murder and not suicide. I had to investigate and find out more details. I just could not give up this now; I had to find out perpetrator behind this. This may open a lid over a bigger conspiracy which perhaps Ankit had planned to uncover.

I went the next day to meet Tanmay at the rehabilitation center. It was a meeting day where guardians could meet their patients. I was relieved to see Tanmay brighter and happier. After enquiring about his health, I showed him the reports. On reading it, Tanmay said, "Our suspicion had been validated. The reports indicate a high possibility of him being murdered. We have to find about how the drugs were being sold online. Just a week before this fateful incident happened he had told me about the drug racket which has an international terrorist nexus which he came to know from a drug supplier. There is one pharmacy company who cheaply supplies these drugs to young children and turns them into addicts. He also talked about confronting them. I feel that this threat led to his death."

I asked, "Then how do we go about this?"

Tanmay said, "Unfortunately I do not know the identity of any one of these. I think we should try to contact the drug peddler first. Through him, we will come to know more details. Ankit used to buy these drugs online, so you should check his laptop to try to find some leads."

I bid him adieu with a promise to come back next week with his parents to meet him.

The Wisdom of Yoga Sutras

We were assembled in the seminar hall of the rehabilitation center. The rectangular hall was decorated in gradient shades of grey with distinctive gold accents. It was specially designed for hosting various performances, video shows, and presentations. The stage backdrop had a banner, "Chaitanya Yoga Society". The program schedule of Rehabilitation center included a weekly featured seminar presented by various distinguished guests. I really liked those talks for they were abundantly insightful not only about addiction but also about life in general. I also realized that hearing from such experts was an essential means of keeping my intellect sharper which was needed to nip the tempting distractions in the bud.

Dr. Vikas introduced the chief guest, "Today we have with us Mr. Nishant Ranganathanji. He is an erudite Sanskrit scholar known all over India for his extensive expertise on the Yoga Sutras. He is also an expert Saroj musician. He lectures on yoga sutra and conducts his musical concerts all over the world. He has learned yoga sutras from a grand-disciple of great yoga teacher Krishnamacharya. He will enlighten us today on the topic of 'How to Change Negative Habits.' Yoga and pranayama are seen as the best means of controlling the mind and keeping the body fit. We specifically have called Ranganathanji to address the audience today. Let us all welcome him!"

Ranganathanji wore a white kurta and a pajama while his hair curled around his nape. He had a beautiful mark- red in the middle of two thick white lines extending from the bridge of his nose to his forehead. Although of wheatish hue and slender form, his limbs were well developed with prominent veins which gave one a distinction of a dedicated practitioner of Yoga. He went on the dais and recited prayers in a clear voice with a hint of a South Indian accent.

He then began, "What is Yoga? Please raise your hands and answer one at a time as I point out"

"It is a way to keep our body healthy."

"Exercises and postures."

"Sleeping peacefully in yoga nidra," someone shouted mischievously.

"Following slim beautiful girls doing exercise," at which many giggled.

"Thank you, guys for the interesting responses especially the last one," he chuckled. "But if we go by the complete definition of yoga, then it is not an exercise nor is it a breathing technique or silent meditation." Pointing his index finger in the air, he said, *Yogah chitta vritti nirodha*- Yoga is calming the patterns of mind. It is very difficult to calm the mind. But yoga helps you do that. Whatever you just mentioned are simply aspects of the process."

He turned to one of the volunteers near the dais "Can you illustrate how we can experience the power of the mind?"

"By concentrating it on one topic and how fast we grasp it demonstrates the power of the mind"

"That's good, anybody else?"

"When we can make a wonderful plan with mind and see it come under reality."

"That's also wonderful, I want few more answers."

Someone at the back of the hall then yelled, "When we mentally experience the psychedelic effects after an acid trip which we never experience in this world." The hall echoed with hearty laughter.

Ranganathanji chided gently, "That's naughty-psychedelic effects don't take much time to become a psychosis- a state of utter confusion and misery, so we should be careful not to fall prey to it. Someone else please try"

"When we are in a depression, we feel disheartened and everything around us feels useless, it is a kind of power of our mind that makes us feel miserable although everything else is nice around us."

Satisfied with the response, the yogi added, "All of these are correct. But I wanted to highlight on one particular definition. We can experience the power of the mind when we try to go against it. In doing so, we can actually experience the power of anything in the world. One can experience the power of the flow of the river while swimming upstream. Let's say when your mind says to enjoy playing a video game but you want to study, and then it becomes really difficult to oppose the mind and do what we want to do. Another example is when you want to get up in the morning but the mind says no, then not obeying mind and doing what is right requires a lot of inner strength.

Generally, most of the people follow their mind without giving any thought to it. However, yoga teaches you to see yourself as different from the mind. The mind is the tool you use but you should not identify yourself with the mind. Hence, sometimes you deny your mind when it is not taking you in a healthy or right direction. We need not take the mind's suggestions so seriously every time they pop up.

The mind is generally clouded by thought patterns. These patterns are called as *Vrittis* which means active thoughts. These thoughts leave an impression on the mind which is called as *Samskar*. These *samskaras* are not visible to us but they are carried over from lifetime after lifetime. When we come in the appropriate atmosphere again; these *samskaras* are aroused, activated and converted into *Vrittis*, which in turn create fresh *samskaras* back in our subconscious mind. *Smriti* or memory causes us to remember our previous *samskaras*. I will give an example to you: When you eat a tasty pizza at a pizza shop, you feel happy. The location of the pizza shop, the shop itself and the pizza, all of these leave a subtle impression on the mind i.e. *Samskar*. When you are in the nearby area and perhaps see the shop, that particular *Samskar* is collected from the mind by way of previous *Smriti* and you experience certain thoughts of enjoying a nice pizza in the shop. These thoughts are called as *vritti*.

This memory is formed by the experience of pleasure. *'Sukhanushayi Ragah'* that which follows the experience of pleasure is called as an attachment. It is a state of mind with agreeable feelings and an inclination towards the locus of pleasure and can only happen when one has earlier experienced that pleasure. The past impressions of that pleasure will bring remembrance of it and strong urges to enjoy it again if one came in contact with the object of that pleasure as the attachment is developed towards the object of that pleasure. This very attachment is the root cause of any habit. Now the object may not give similar pleasure as one experienced earlier, however, the stored impressions *(samskaras)* will bring back the memory of past pleasure and induce one to try to enjoy that pleasure again.

This is the root cause of addiction. These impressions or *vrittis* could be erased when yoga is achieved. Yoga Sutra says *"yogas chitta vritti nirodha"*.

When you develop positive impressions gradually by yoga, old impressions are relegated to the background or erased permanently. Thus, by forming good positive impressions, one can come out of negative bad habits and cultivate good positive habits.

"Interesting," I said and asked, "Could you explain how to do that through yoga?"

Another meaning of yoga comes from root '*Yuj*' in Sanskrit which means to connect. We recommend connecting with spiritual sounds which called '*Naad Brahma*' as a means to cleanse the mind. The Yoga Sutra says, '*Taj japas tad artha bhavanam*'-Through repetition, the meaning of the chants becomes clear. For this age, the simplest form of yoga which is recommended is the musical repetition of spiritual chants.

Yoga is music. Music has a lot of power and so we recommend using music for the elevation of consciousness. Ancient mantras are specifically potent with the energy which has to be experienced. When accompanied by musical instruments, we can experience that potency even faster. I recently met Dr. David Brian Wolf who did doctorate research on the effect of ancient spiritual chants. This research indicated that these sound vibrations have scientifically been proven successful in the treatment of stress, depression, and addictions. So when you are in touch with such sound vibrations; gradually your old impressions are erased and you form a new positive impression. In my concerts, I have seen people who were sad and depressed when they came in, were in complete bliss as we progressed with our Musical mantra show.

This is something like antivirus software- the negative thoughts patterns and impressions are like viruses which are erased after you install the anti-virus software and automatically your computer becomes more efficient. Similarly, through these sound vibrations, your mind becomes pure and efficient. Our grand spiritual teacher Krishnamacharya was an expert at reciting these spiritual chants."

Following this lengthy and enlightening speech, questions and answers continued for another hour. One boy asked, "My mind always wanders during meditation sessions. How can I control it?"

Ranganathanji replied, "The Yoga Sutra says, *'Abhyasa vairagyabhyam tan nirodhah'*. These mental disturbances are restrained by practice and detachment. We need to regularly practice meditation and we have to practice to bring the mind back to the object of meditation. The mind is like a small child who will run off and we need to practice to bring it back to the object of our meditation.

It is interesting that focusing the mind on the *Vishaya* i.e. object of senses- Rupa, Gandha, Rasa, Sparsha, Dhvani (sight, odor, taste, touch, sound) brings attachment and suffering. So we have to practice detachment from these sense objects. When the same mind is focused on spiritual matters, it gets purified of all the impurities.

"Sir, but the cravings are so strong, how is it possible to overcome them?"

He raised his stubby index finger and said, "By higher taste. The higher taste of the meditation will create indifference towards the cravings. In fact, during the advanced stages you would crave for even higher meditational pleasure which doesn't have any side effect nor does it dissipate with time. It takes some time but one has to persevere to achieve these higher meditations. Also, by dwelling the mind of the philosophical truths, the *Viveka* or discernment will increase. By the power of this *Viveka* we can stay away from harmful cravings. That's why we recommend our students to regularly study philosophical literature to understand the true nature of the world.

Yoga Sutra defines Avidya as '*Antiya Asuchi duhkha anatmasu nitya shuchi sukha atman khyatih avidya*' As per this definition the Ignorance (*avidya*) is of four types:

1. Regarding that which is temporary as permanent. (Anitya Nitya)
2. Mistaking the impure for pure (Asuchi suchi)
3. Thinking that which brings misery to bring happiness (duhkha sukha) and
4. Taking that which is not-self to be self (Anatma atman).

In this way, you will see our cravings can have power over us only when we are ignorant. We consider the happiness given by fulfilment of those cravings as permanent happiness, although it is very momentary and we consider it great, although it produced misery later. We think it as the most pleasurable thing and though such cravings are not part of our real nature, we will think of them as our own hankerings. So by studying the philosophical literature, one can rise above such cravings."

"Sir", one person raised his hand in the back. "Sir, why it is so difficult to cultivate new good habits?"

"Because most of the healthy habits give you happiness in long-term while in short term it is not so pleasurable. So there are no pleasurable samskaras for good habits during the short term. We have to intellectually understand its importance and continue doing it even though we don't derive pleasure from it at first. For example, most people do not like to study but those who persevere and study always get better results and it gives them further impetus for studies. We should also refrain from people, places and things which provoke our earlier wrong *Samskaras* because, in such a company, it will be difficult for us to not be tempted."

Another boy asked, "Do we have to give up seeing, hearing everything which is enjoyable to avoid pleasurable *samskaras*?"

Ranganathanji replied, "You needn't give up everything. Just use this thumb rule: 'Whether the impression created from this thing would be good or harmful to me in the longer term?' We can assess the quality of our impressions based on whether they facilitate our meditation or distract us. There is no harm in accepting those inputs which are useful for our meditation. The sensory inputs that we take, specifically what we hear and read, create ideas in our mind which shape our worldview and we act as per that. Having the right inputs results in a perfect worldview, as all our words, actions, interactions, and expectations are based on this worldview. We see so much suffering, confusion, disagreement and mistrust in the world due to people's improper worldviews. Thus, I would like to conclude with a quote by Wayne Dyer- 'When we change to look at things, the things we look at change.'"

We were deeply enlightened by the philosophical concepts taught by Ranganathanji. I had enough food for thought for days ahead.

Swami in the Hippie Land

One more week in the rehab center was over. This was my last week now. I really had become a better person and I could see a substantial change in myself which gave me great confidence. I had now even started inspiring new patients which were admitted in fresh batches every week.

For this week's special guest lecture, Dr. Vikas introduced the speaker, "We have a special guest among us today who has come from the United States of America. His name is Jim Siegel. Let us welcome him today to Sharanam"

The announcement was followed by applause when the audience settled, he gave a further introduction, "and the guest is the author of the book 'The flipside of sixties and the Swami'. He has recently released this book and today he is going to talk about this book with us. He has introduced in his book intimate tales of 1960s iconic figures and events. He depicts a trajectory of his experience during that time which is distinctively counter-cultural, American and radical. Also included are his experiences with drugs, relationships and traveling. The most amazing thing among all this is that he came in touch with one Indian swami who transformed his life and got a permanent connection with India. He also participated in the civil right movement marches of

USA under Dr. Martin Luther King. He is currently leading a number of projects for supporting weaker sections of society. His talk will be followed by question and answers. Let's welcome him here."

Tall, white-skinned Jim had an oval face beaming with a smile. He appeared handsome still in his sixties which indicated he must have been a very handsome man in his youth. He wore a striped light gray Indian kurta with pajama trousers. His gray-white hair was parted in middle and he had a broad smile as if he appeared to be excited to do something wonderful. He thanked the organizers in his heavily accented English intermixed with a few Hindi phrases.

"Namaste! Since I am at a rehabilitation center, today I am going to specifically speak about my plentiful experiences with drugs. I lived my youth in the peak of the drug era in the USA so I hope you will relate with my experiences and also learn a few good things. I was raised in New York City. My father was a successful insurance agent. After leaving my school, I aimlessly floundered on the lower east side of Bowery for some time before I joined a New English School for Social Research. After that, I joined as a tutor for deprived children at Harlem. The purpose of the program was to educate them which spawned the current 'No One Left behind' Act of the government.

There I met Chickie who was assisting us. He was a natural leader. One day he came to our meeting, he had been taking heroin and he wanted to stop. He said, "I want to stop but it's so hard, and it's out there and available, it feels so good for a while, but then so bad and so expensive. Sometimes I have to resort to crime to keep up my habit. Please help me stop taking heroin."

I asked Chickie to move in with me away from the distraction of heroin dealers. I told him, "I had an experience of putting people through cold turkey - abrupt cessation of the drug from the people who are already taking it. He agreed, "No matter what I say, no matter how much I plead, don't let me go back."

The next week together we went through cold sweats and hot fevers, him desperately pleading before throwing up. I had to lock us in when he tried to bolt out of the apartment. I would bring him blankets when he was getting the chills, and then he would throw them off when he was feeling feverish, fists clenched writhing on the bed. Patiently I was there. After four days, he was pacing, resting and finally eating. Gradually he overcame his addiction. It took me a lot of effort and dedication to help him become sober.

I narrated this incident to acknowledge how difficult this recovery program is but one should always take support and still persist in enduring these difficulties.

I was inspired by personalities like Bob Dylan who wanted to bring solutions to problems not from a political perspective but through arts and music. I heard Charlie Jones singing 'We shall overcome' against discrimination which propelled me to go to down south to Birmingham, Alabama and participate in the civil right movement. After that, I participated in many protest marches and even went to jail for the same.

In my own life, I had also experimented with drugs. After Harlem, I went on a tour in Mexico. I met Dr. Timothy Leary at Ajijic Mexico. He had been experimenting with LSD and he proposed that if it is used wisely, it could change the world. He propagated the idea of expansion of mind and consciousness through LSD.

I was inspired by him and I took a few LSD doses. I was looking for an ultimate groove, the nth degree, the zenith. I grew to enjoy the lifestyle but became tolerant to the drugs. I needed new experiences, but there were no new ones. Getting high again and again was not enough. I was looking for the ultimate high, within and without. The less I needed, the happier I could be. I was searching for the most natural and eternal high. At that time I landed in San Francisco.

Later I met my girlfriend and would be wife Joan. She was extremely smart and talented at cooking, singing, calligraphy. One day her sister came with her boyfriend named Mike from Brooklyn. Mike shared with us amazing tale of an Indian swami who played an important role for de-addiction of hippies of America at the most crucial time of counter culture. He touched my life too. I got a purpose to live by associating myself with him. So I am going to share what Mike said about his New York experiences with Swami and my experiences with Swami.

First, let me tell you the background of counter-culture movement. By 1965, the lower east side of New York was abuzz with hundreds and thousands of youth migrated from all over the USA, dwelling in the slums. They migrated there because of the cheap rent. At first, the newcomers were mostly young artists, musicians, and intellectuals. Then came the young middle-class dropouts. Many even came without finding a place to live and camped in the hallways of tenements. Drawn by the cheap rent and the promise of Bohemian freedom, these young middle-class dropouts soon to be known in the media as "hippies," and were deemed as against America's ideal life of materialism.

The hippies journeyed to the Lower East Side of Newyork turning away from the suburban materialism of their parents, the inane happiness of TV and advertising-the ephemeral goals of middle-class America. They were disillusioned and allured by radical political ideologies that exposed America as a cruel, selfish, exploitative giant who must now reform or die. And they were searching for real love, real peace, real existence, and real spiritual consciousness. I see now in India also some of the youths are getting disillusioned.

The first front in the great youth rebellion of the sixties had already entered the Lower East Side. Here they were free-free to live in simple poverty and express themselves through art, music, drugs, and sex. The talk was of spiritual searching. LSD and marijuana were the keys, opening new realms of awareness. Notions about Eastern cultures and Eastern religions were in vogue. They though through drugs, yoga, brotherhood, or just by being free-somehow they would attain enlightenment. Everyone was supposed to keep an open mind and develop his own cosmic philosophy by direct experience and drug-expanded consciousness, blended with his own eclectic readings.

So it was that in 1966, thousands of young people were walking the streets of the Lower East Side, not simply intoxicated or crazy (though they often were), but in search of life's ultimate answers, in complete disregard of "the establishment" and the day-to-day life pursued by millions of "straight" Americans.

Incidentally or by some divine arrangement, seventy years old Indian Swami Bhaktivedanta happened to be staying in the same place. He represented eastern culture and philosophy and he had come there to distribute it in the west. Swami traveled an arduous journey in his old age suffering two heart attacks while traveling through a rough sea in 1965. He came alone, with the sole purpose of sharing the message of India with the western world. He knew nobody, he didn't know where to go or stay, he had practically no money, and he just came with a trunk full of books of Indian philosophical literature translated by him. He landed in New York in the lower east side. After an initial struggle for almost a year, he got a storefront for conducting his programs.

Among the program goers there were few who had regular job and lifestyle also but in the beginning, most of them were hippies. The main program was lunch. Initially, Swami would himself cook for all his students and even wash their plates and pots. Later his regular students would go out and shop, getting donations whenever possible, for whole wheat flour, garbanzo flour, split peas, rice, and whatever vegetables were cheap or free. Then every day the cooks would prepare spiced mashed potatoes, buttered chapattis, split-pea dal, and a vegetable dish—for two hundred people.

The lunch program was possible because many merchants were willing to donate to the recognized cause of feeding hippies. The hippies would be really hungry. The people would just all huddle together, and we would really line them up against the wall to wall. A lot of them would simply eat and leave. But we were welcoming everybody. We were providing a kind of refuge from the tumult and madness of the street scene. So it was in that sense a hospital, and I think a lot of people were helped and maybe even saved. I don't mean only their souls—I mean their minds and bodies were saved, because of what was going on in the streets that they just simply couldn't handle. I'm talking about overdoses of drugs, people who were plain lost and needed comforting and who sort of wandered or staggered into the temple.

There was much public concern about the huge influx of youth, a situation that was creating an almost uncontrollable social problem. Police and welfare workers were worried about health problems and poor living conditions, especially. Some middle-class people feared a complete hippie take over. The local authorities welcomed the service offered by Swami Bhaktivedanta's center.

In one of the famous talks on addiction, Johann Hari says, "Opposite of addiction is not sobriety. The opposite of addiction is a connection." He gave them connection and engagement which made them sober. He spent time with them. He gave them a practical lifestyle of getting up early in the morning, participating in morning services followed by sumptuous, tasty and healthy food. After this program in the morning, he engaged them in a variety of ways as per their talents like cooking, painting, mentoring, public singing, cultivating farms, editing, publishing and distributing literature, conducting famous Indian cart festival parades in western cities etc. These engagements along with a pure lifestyle purified them of all the bad tendencies.

He wrote a great number of books and lectured extensively and everything became crystal clear. Even they tried to enjoy drugs etc. it was not the same. They realized actually they were searching something which they already possessed within. They were experiencing much deeper shelter in him than the flimsy shelter that the drugs offered. They were vulnerable to their own bad habits, flaws in their character and wrong company around but they came out of that because they submitted themselves to his guidance.

And everyone was appreciative, especially the young people. Swami was always available for them. Anybody could go and meet him in his rooms. He was like an encyclopedia who knew something about everything.

Just from a medical standpoint, doctors didn't know what to do with people on LSD. The police and the free clinics in the area couldn't handle the overload of people taking LSD. The police saw Swamiji as a certain refuge. He had an amazing ability through devotion to get people off drugs, especially speed, heroin, burnt-out LSD cases—all of that.

He was getting appreciations like:

"Swami Bhaktivedanta is close to 100% successful in stopping drug use among those who voluntarily enter the program"—Addictions Magazine, Washington, D.C, Area Council on Alcoholism & Drug Abuse.Inc."

"You have done good work in establishing a workable alternative to the problem of drug addiction and alienation."—Morris Jeff, New Orleans Welfare Director.

"Mayor Lindsay is most appreciative of the work that your Society is doing, especially in the realm of combating drug addiction"—Woody Klein, Press Secretary, Office of the Mayor, City of New York.

Swami said, "It is practical experience in the USA the government is spending millions of dollars for stopping this intoxication habit amongst the younger generation. But the wonderful thing is they inquire also from us that as soon as they come to us, immediately gives up. Why? That is the special prerogative of our movement"

The Indian traditional Swami and American hippie, there couldn't exist stark difference between two individuals in terms of culture, age, experience, wisdom and orientation of life as it was existing between these two. He worked in such a different setting from his own for saving American hippies.

For hippies along with food, he would hold public chants in the Tompkins square park, Absorbed in singing while sitting down and playing his bongo drum. The hippies participated singing and dancing encircling him. Very soon many of the hippies actually joined him leaving behind all their bad habits of drug smacking, promiscuity etc. It was a great miracle, even the government was amazed. In the very short time of ten years, his young students grew from numbers which could be counted on fingers to thousands. They all had embraced the clean, pure lifestyle.

He after his initial success had come to San Francisco. It is where I first met him and started attending his meetings. I had never seen a person like him anywhere in the world. He was completely absorbed in something divine beyond the world. His teachings conveyed the essence of everything I had learned in Jewish faith Torah and Kabbalah, along with Zen Buddhist Koans and sutras, the Bushido code, Taoism and Native American wisdom. He would get up around 1:30 AM in the morning. He would chant on his beads names of Krishna and he translated books from Sanskrit to English in early morning hours. In this way in the very short span of life, he transformed the lives of thousands of Westerners to a purer way of living.

His teachings have the power to bring enlightenment which would help one to understand how one gets trapped in addictions and how they should tackle it. So I wish to share a few of his teachings.

He shared as per teachings of devotional philosophy; we are all spiritual beings at our core. Spiritual existence is eternal, all cognizant and blissful. The urge to be happy comes from our own inherent nature to be always happy as spiritual beings. But when that state is forgotten and one simply identifies with material things in life then one experiences pain and misery.

You know people judge themselves by how they look, what car they possess or where they stay. But all these things are relative and subject to change. If our sense of self comes from identification with such materialistic things then we are sure to feel hurt and broken when they are gone. Even if they remain same, the satisfaction derived from them will only decrease with our every attempt to enjoy them as in the economics they state the law of diminishing marginal utility.

The urge to dull or distort one's awareness using drugs comes from a sense of futility and hopelessness. The reductionist understanding of life, limiting it to a bunch of elements of material nature and forgetfulness of spirit behind results in negative worldview about life. Such understanding neglects the higher aspect of and respect for life. Life rather than seen as divine blessings is seen as just an outcome of elements of material nature.

What happens when you don't have respect for something?"

Kathy from Kerala replied in her verbose English, "We don't utilize that thing properly. I have seen stinking rich wards in my class who had no value for money, they were spendthrifts. But those who were coming from the humble economic background, their parsimony were displayed by their careful expenditure. We can even see from old historic sites, having no respect for them, litterbugs have destroyed their beauty"

"Thank you, Kathy, similar to this example we can see that bearing disrespectful attitude towards life devalues it and people don't care about using it for right cause in the right way. And the sense of emptiness, futility, and hopelessness pervades. People try to deal with that emptiness by taking drugs. The cigarette in hand is seen as a prestige symbol.

So when there is no ultimate goal and if you have achieved all your material goals then why will you want to live your life ahead? What would be the purpose? It would be very empty. Since everything here has beginning and end. So a sensitive child can understand that life in this world is basically miserable and temporary. And if the present life is everything, with nothing beyond death and gross matter, why not create a more pleasant reality - at least within one's mind? That's the reason people get high on drugs. They want to create a pleasant picture of reality at-least in their minds.

So this quest of getting high is characteristics of a living being. Essentially we all are pleasure seekers. But in the absence of knowledge of what is a real pleasure, we accept cheap material pleasures as all in all.

Swami appeared to be situated in something very high. Ordinary situations did not disturb him and his determination. He had tremendous faith which enabled him to transcend the limitations of the body. He was working twenty hours a day at the age of eighty while his young disciples in twenties could not catch up with him. He never faced jet lags or boredom etc. He was always available for service despite his health conditions. But he never did it with frustration; he was always jolly while doing everything he did.

When we asked him, "how could you do so? How we could acquire your qualities?"

He quoted predecessor teachers in his line, they wrote heaps of highly ornamented Sanskrit literature. Sleeping hardly an hour or two, and eating simple chickpeas, they were the greatest scholars of that time blissfully absorbed in their personal meditations. Even now there are departments in Indian Universities named after them for researching their literatures . He asked, "How could they function so much with such minimum possession?" we were blank. He replied, "Because they had realized their real self which is beyond this material realm. Our real self has an unlimited capacity to experience pleasure when it is immersed in its original function. They were functioning on that plane.

Our senses become sharp by pure spiritual engagements and we can experience higher pleasure exponentially even in the simple things of the world. In the opposite way, sense indulgence blunts our senses and we lose taste in whatever we are doing and we need higher doses of enjoyment to feel the same amount of pleasure again."

I asked, "But what about people who take to addiction because of the turmoil they are going through and they need to forget that?"

"When the effect of drug vanishes, the severity of turmoil experienced is many folds. So the calmness produced by drugs is varieties of illusion or delusion only. But spirituality teaches how to transcend the turmoil by our elevated consciousness and how to sail over that kind of storms in life rather than somehow trying to run away from them by artificial consciousness adulteration. In such cases, people go on increasing their doses. Fourteen percent of the population from my country died last year of a drug overdose. We just have ten more minutes to close; I will take two last questions"

"How could you trust somebody so much that you gave your lives for him, especially when he was a foreigner to you?" asked a person, he had become an addict because he couldn't deal with his boss.

"We tested him. Some people even stealthily put the camera in his apartment to know what he does when he was alone. But he was nothing but sincere. There were no incongruities in his life. He was same inside and outside. His compassion touched us. We had a notion that times 'don't trust anybody above thirty', but this old man stole our hearts with his love. We realized we needed him because without his help we would never know what would please God; he represented God's compassion in our lives. He empowered us so much so that within a short time of few years his teachings spread all over the world.

He opened more than 100 centers or I would rather say rehabilitation centers in the context of this place, across the world because most of his followers' experience says that they gave up on drugs and all sort of intoxications after coming in touch with the Swami. One of step in 12 steps program explains true recovery means not only giving up intoxications but also character defects which come along with it. Now continuing his legacy, his students run around more than 5000 weekly meetings all over the world to help people deal with their character defects and develop higher taste in personal and group meditations which have helped lakhs of people become sober truly from the core of their beings."

The talk was interrupted by a huge round of applause. We were all inspired by Swami's work.

"Sir, after hearing about this Indian Swami, we are really inspired to know more about him, can you please share your most memorable events with Swami?"

"I have multiple, I will share three short and most interesting with you. Once one hippie asked Swami, what it is like happiness in the abode of God."

Swami Replied, "It is like an ocean of LSD." Swami knew how to connect with us so that we grabbed what he wanted to say for us. He attracted us by speaking in our language.

Some other time, seeing the problems in the world and USA, I said to swami, "sometimes I feel bad seeing the situation of the world"

Swamiji said, "Why only sometimes?" He had immense compassion.

When Swami was in England, somebody asked him, "why did you come from India to here?"

Swami had participated in Gandhi's movement in his youth, he said, "You Britishers, you looted everything valuable from India. But you forgot to take with you, the most valuable thing that is the spiritual culture of India. I have come here to give you that."

At the end of the talk guest, Mr. Jim sponsored few free copies of philosophical literature. I quickly grabbed a couple of them.

Part III

Stealthy Route

My one month stay in the rehabilitation center had been the most enlightening period of my life. I had formed a great relationship with many of my batch-mates. The various speakers like yoga teacher Nishant and Jim had made a deep transformation to the ways in which I was thinking and doing things. Regular meditation, spiritual sounds; exercise became part of daily life. By reading books shared by Jim, I developed insights to deal with day to day situations of my life. These all gifts gave me a sense of fulfillment and nourishment in my life which helped me to get out of the urges I occasionally felt.

Now I knew whom I can turn to when I am in dire need of help. Friendship with people like Larry was an asset. I was in touch with 'Sharanam' through regular attendance in their periodically arranged programs.

It was 7 AM in the morning when my phone rang. I was in a half-slumber while I picked up, it was Aarya.

"I did tons of research for a past few days and stayed up late night and got some valuable pointers which could help us in further investigating Ankit's death. I couldn't even sleep properly last night. I have been going through a very restless phase all this time and so I couldn't stop myself from calling you early this morning."

I said, "What kind of leads are you talking about so early in the morning?"

"Leads regarding online drug peddling network which is being operated here. We will meet regarding the same, would you mind a meeting at our home?" she asked.

"Ok, shall we meet at our place by morning 11 am?" I said.

She said, "That's perfect".

I went to her house and everything was the same at their house except there was gloominess in the atmosphere. I wondered which parents in the world can tolerate such kind of sorrow. They must be intensely suffering. I noticed a pleasant smell arriving from the hallways and there was a big picture of Ankit hung in the hall room with a colorful garland on it.

Ankit's mother, therefore, my aunt welcomed me and offered me snacks and water. She had dark circles under her eyes and they'd puffed and swollen to the extent which made it clear she'd been shedding tears for a past few days incessantly, and didn't have sufficient sleep for months.

I asked, "Aunty, how are you? You seem so completely disarrayed",

"I have no words to convey son. Your bosom friend Ankit was very dear to me even when he got himself involved in such matters. His absence is so strongly felt here and it is intolerable. Why is God so cruel? Why a mother does have to experience the mourning of her own child's death, Could he not take me before he took my child?" she wailed.

Uncle interrupted, "Why blame God for our mistakes? A man gets fruits of his own deeds. When Ankit wanted our time, we were busy making money. We thought we were the best parents to give him all the facilities he needed but barely did we spare our time for him, we gave him everything in terms of things but never looked upon to satisfy his emotional needs. So, when he needed us he found our money, not us. We could not establish a strong connection with him. He required our help when he found himself around drugs and as we substituted our presence with bank balances for him; all he did was buy some of the drugs which helped him fill in the gaps. Had we been a little less busy, he would not have fallen into the trap of those deadly drugs. Don't you see it's our mistake?

Whatever you sow so shall you reap. Although we were poor, my parents made sure that they trained me properly. My father was a farmer and mother was a simple housewife. My father would take me to the farm when I would be free and that is where I got some practical skills and engagements along with my regular education. My mother taught me prayers, told me stories from scriptures. She would ask me to water the holy Tulsi plant every day and I just wish, if we could be so proactive for our son. My parents made sure we had our dinner together. I forgot all this and went only behind the career but I face such heartburn now." I did not understand.

His mom said "It's true, we lacked responsibility while rearing our child and now we face this great melancholy. I wipe tears away in grief. Son, you were Ankit's best friend. Do visit us come here regularly; it brings me great solace when I see you. I see my son in you."

I said, "Surely Auntie, Today, I have come here regarding some important work with Aarya. And I would definitely stay back for lunch. I would do anything to have your pain eased."

"It's our privilege son, never be shy to meet us. See this as your other home and please keep coming."

I had snacks and after that, I continued with Aarya.

She said, "I have found some good leads which may help us."

"What did you discover?" I asked.

Pulling back her long hair she said, "I have found out how drugs are sold over the dark web on the internet. I feel we definitely can get some clue with this information."

"Could you please explain more?" I asked.

She said, "If you think of the web like an iceberg, you have the surface web up top. It's the internet you see and use every day and consists of all the websites indexed by traditional search engines like Google. What's submerged in the deep web — an anonymous online space only accessible with specific software. The Deep Web refers to any website that cannot be readily accessed through any conventional search engine. The reason for this is because the content has not been indexed by the search engine in question.

"Then what is dark web?" I asked.

"Dark Web or Darknet is a subset of the Deep Web where there are sites that sell drugs, hacking software, counterfeit money and more. It lies within the deepest points of the internet abyss."

I asked, "How do we access it then?"

"One of the most popular software I mentioned to access the dark web is tor.

Tor actually works you need to know what happens when you typically search the web. Think of your IP address as an online identity. Each time you visit a website, you can be traced back to your exact location thanks to that IP address.

The Tor browser looks like any other, except that there's a whole lot happening that you don't see. Instead of your connection request bouncing from its origin right to its destination, Tor sends your request on a much more roundabout route.

Let's say you're in Mumbai and you want to search a site hosted in Delhi. Instead of connecting you directly, the Tor browser takes you on at least three random detours called relays. Your request could go from Mumbai to South Africa, from South Africa to Hong Kong and from Hong Kong to Delhi.

So the user of the dark web cannot be tracked from where he is accessing the internet. And it keeps the user secret, so people use the tor browser."

"It is really dark out there; does nobody use it for a good purpose?" I asked

"The dark net is also used for better things by the journalists, political whistleblowers, people from oppressed countries etc.", she said, "We could search Ankit's browser history since he used to buy them online."

We turned on his laptop. Generally, TOR browser deletes all the user data after being shut down. We prayed and prayed for the laptop to not be shut down and tor browser closed on it. Fortunately, the laptop was on hibernation mode, we switched it on and tor browser opened in it. The e-shop window was open. We planned to order from it. We placed an order of meth drug on the online store waiting for it to be delivered.

The Peddler's Story

Three days after ordering the drugs from the online store, my phone rang. It was one of the supply agents,

"Is it Tanmay Bendale?" I said, "Yes."

"Sir your parcel is ready, when will you be available?'

I didn't know what I felt on hearing this but I replied hurriedly, "Yes, I'm available. By what time will you reach here?"

He didn't miss a beat and almost immediately told me that he'd be here in some fifteen minutes.

The bell rang after a while.

I opened the door.

There was a person standing in front of the door. He was a stout and heavy man with a dark complexion. His eyes were hidden behind pitch black sunglasses with 'Ray Ban' inscribed at one of the corners. His leather jacket didn't reveal much of his huge body which was covered with a thin white and black tee.

But the only thing I could think about at this moment, staring at the heavy silver chains hanging around his wrist, was the hefty amount this person standing in front of me must get paid for being a mere delivery man. There was a bulky looking backpack leaning by his leg. I assumed he delivered to many places, just like he did mine.

I had to exchange codes with him as a recognition procedure to keep the transaction airtight.

As I disclosed my code to him, he pulled out a ziplock pouch from one of the compartments in his bulky looking bag. It contained the tablets I had ordered; 10 gm of meth in form of tablets. A quick smile left my lips as I hurriedly took the pouch from him and handed the cash over.

He turned around towards his bike but before I could help, the thought left my mouth as I asked him, "You look completely drained, would you like a glass of water?"

He looked at me and nodded.

I went back to the house and seized a glass, poured some water in and added a few ice cubes then rushed towards the front door.

I handed over the glass while he took off his Ray-Bans revealing bloodshot eyes and dark bags underneath. He looked like he was on drugs himself and not just distributing them. He started gulping down the water when I hesitantly asked him, "Do you know Ankit? Ankit Malhotra?"

He looked surprised and answers my question with another question, "How do you know him?"

I waited for a while before replying, "He was my best friend. His sudden departure, it still disturbs me. Did you know him?"

He looked away before answering me, "I knew

him for a very long time. I used to supply to him and his friends".

I considered this as an opportunity to find out about all he knew about Ankit, "Would you like to have some snacks and a little chat with me?"

He agreed.

I welcomed him to my house. He entered at once and made himself comfortable on our sofa. I asked my mother to prepare some snacks to keep him occupied for a little longer; after all, he was one of our leads to Ankit's murder.

"Generally, I do not wait for a long time at an unknown place. But since you are Ankit's friend, I came in. I knew him for the past many years. I worked as a bartender before at the Diamond club where he frequented with his parents for parties. We were quick to become friends from mere acquaintances. He was a very amicable person. He would drink with his friends, some of whom were junkies and complete addicts; they often pushed him to try chemicals."

I got the feeling that he was still a little out of it because the ease with which he was giving out all the information wouldn't be possible if he was absolutely in a sober condition.

He kept going, "...Ankit was a little uneasy with it, didn't really want to get himself involved in it but he could not withstand the pressure his friends created on him to try it out. I served at that club every day. Saw most of the exchanges and couldn't really control my curiosity. So I gave in and tried it myself a few times. And here I am, addicted. Gradually my need increased and I couldn't afford drugs with just the job of a bartender.

Eventually, I started selling drugs and roping in new people to have them as well. The main dealer had an offer. For every new customer, I'd bring, I'd get a free dose. This was all I had to do to satisfy my needs, so I did it without another thought, fishing out a new customer every week to keep myself from getting charged for drugs. And Ankit was just one of the customers."

He finished and then turned his attention towards me.

"What about you? Why are you asking me about him?"

"I was his friend. I knew he was into doping, therefore I asked you about him. Did you guys ever discuss personal matters with each other?"

"Ankit had a very kind heart. There are only a few customers who would come to you and want to know about your life. He was one of them. His heart ached to see the destitute.

Whenever we sat down for a talk I would share my life situations with him. We became friends. I suffered from my financial problems and Ankit mostly lamented about feeling lonely and complained that his family never really spared time for him; they just stashed him with money or other expensive presents.

They were never really there for him. He used to say *'I don't want presents, I want presence.'* We both were dealing with our own frustrations. And when we were given an opportunity to ease away our pain and struggle, maybe even just for a moment. Just a temporary relief, we took it! We took it, and that was our mistake.

Temporary relief, that's what we believed it, was. I still feel I shouldn't be here supplying drugs and consuming them after what it cost to Ankit. But I'm bound to it. My will to give up drugs at this point of addiction is not as strong as the need for it to bear the suffering it causes me when I miss my doses.

I wish I hadn't tried it, ever. I wish I had lived with my miseries for a few more months, I wished we both had a little more strength to avoid it, My friends and relatives wouldn't have had turned their back on me, I wouldn't have been such an outcast in my society. My parents wouldn't be cursing upon me because of all the shame I brought upon them in their life. Things would have been much easier. I wouldn't have to worry about managing enough money to buy drugs, wouldn't have to lie and keep making excuses.

But at last, we both planned to stop this entirely rather than our own stimulated once in while tries which failed mostly, therefore, we thought of enrolling in a rehab center. He was generous enough to sponsor at the Rehabilitation center for my recovery."

"I heard that he was frustrated with all such problems and wanted to end his life? Did he discuss any such matters with you? Do you think he could have had taken his own life?"

"Well, under such influence people tend to speak about matters which are irrelevant and after a drug trip, it brings enough depression to people that they might actually think of giving up their life but a person needs a higher motive to actually go through with it. As far as I knew Ankit, he wouldn't do such a thing, I mean why would he take his own life when he planned for both of ours' enrollment at the Rehab Center?"

"When was the last time you saw him?" I asked, "What did you discuss with him?"

He hesitated for a moment but then answered anyway.

"Please do not tell anybody. I am sharing only with you because you are Ankit's close friend.

I was under an acid trip that day when he came to meet me. I was high and unaware of what was happening. I must have blabbered out all the drug routes and chains that I knew of, in my half unconscious state. I had overheard that somebody across the border was hatching a plan to destroy the aspiring youth of this country by facilitating a drug distribution to the colleges of youth.

Our drug handler was being facilitated by forces across the border, as I overheard at our factory. He had high regards for this nation and he wanted to trace it out. He told that he himself would volunteer for the task but it was our last meeting and I never met him. My father is in his critical state of cancer and my handler is supplying money for the treatment so although it's against my will and ethics I have to work for him, I'm bound to.

So please don't ask me anything further. I should not have told you any of this but you're someone close to Ankit. Please do not disclose this to anybody. I am still bound to this web for my father's treatment."

"I won't tell anybody but I need to find out the exact cause for his death for I suspect it to be a murder and not suicide. If you can tell me the name and address of your drug handler, I will carry out the investigation further without involving the police."

"I am sorry but I can't help you with that. I myself am dependent on this whole chain so I am compelled to keep this information. I hope you understand. But if you need any help, apart from this, please let me know."

"Okay, you have helped me enough on your part. I deeply appreciate it."

We exchanged numbers as he left.

Intrusion

"Aarya, we are still not aware of the location of the place where the drugs are manufactured, we must find it out," Tanmay wasn't happy with the way things weren't progressing.

I was frustrated myself as well, "But what's the way, the peddler is not ready to share his address. It is really annoying me. If we chased him, he may come to know about it and never come back."

After much deliberation, we settled on an alternate plan.

We ordered drugs from the online store again. After a few days, the same agent came. He was familiar to him this time so when Tanmay called him in and gave him snacks; he did so without saying anything.

While he was busy munching his snack, Tanmay stealthily put a GPS device inside his bike to track his whereabouts once he left. It was important to find out the pharmaceutical company owner because from there we could get an important lead to his murder.

After a little chit chat, the peddler left.

We turned on the tracking device which tracked him wherever he was going. While we tracked him we found he was visiting a lot of other places that same evening. Later on the map, we found that he went to a pharmaceutical company and from there he went to a place and stayed in the same location for the whole night, probably his home.

We checked the details of the pharmaceutical company he went to, online. The company was under the joint directorship and it had few people working in it. Company manufactured certain drugs.

"Aarya, now we know his location, how should we proceed?" Tanmay asked me.

I said, "I will visit that company under some pretext."

Later, I visited the pharmaceutical company disguised as a research student with a companion who was well-versed in pharmaceuticals. It was a two-story building with a wide expanse on the outskirts of the city. The ground floor seemed to have all the machinery used for drug manufacturing and the godowns and the top floor seemed to be their administrative area. A guard stopped us at the entrance.

After noting our purpose of coming there, he called the manager to meet us.

We asked the manager if we could have a quick sneak peek at the medicines he had in stock, and it's manufacturing, for we needed it for our recent project. He seemed reluctant but just to be nice with us he further asked,

"What do you want to study?"

"Sir, we want to see your production process."

"No sorry, here we manufacture hazardous

chemicals, so we do not quite entertain many outsiders, we cannot allow you. You may search for another company."

"Sir, if you suggest any security measures, we are ready to follow them."

He was adamant and didn't want us to enter inside. While I was busy arguing with the manager for permission to enter the factory, my friend sneaked in and did some quick observations. She saw there were many female workers who were mostly responsible for the cleanliness and hygiene about the place. She quickly noted down one of their mobile numbers.

We were sent back and not allowed to enter, so we left the premises. Later we called up the worker that had given us her number. We decided to meet up with her at her place.

The worker lived in an old shack with her family. She would complete all the household chores in the morning and then leave for her job. We explained to her how to click pictures and somehow convinced her to take some pictures of the premises she cleans every day.

We met her again after two days. She had pictures of every detail of the work she did at that place. We paid her a full month's salary and told her that one of our ladies would replace her in the work at the company. We asked her to speak to her housekeeping supervisor at the company to give permission for replacing her.

"Why you want to do this?" she asked.

"I'm sorry, but we cannot disclose it to you. Our work is of utmost urgency and the information must remain confidential. I hope you will understand our situation and cooperate with us. If you do so, we will pay you three times the money you get as a salary for the job there."

She thought for a while. Her eyes were already lit up with the prospect of getting three times of the money she was earning for the same job.

"Will that not put me in any kind of problem? And you need to pay for everything in advance!" She hesitated but at the same time, she made it clear that money meant more to her than safety.

We assured her, "No, there won't be any problems, you will be alright. You won't even need that job ever again; we will find you a better job than your current one and with a hike in salary, just don't tell this to your supervisor now."

"What should I tell him then?"

"Just tell him, that you need to be away from the city for 2 months and in that period, one of your relatives will replace you."

She was a little confused yet keen to help us with the price she was getting paid. She didn't know why we were doing what we were doing but she accepted the offer. She did as we instructed her to and I joined as a housekeeping staff in her place.

It was too much for me, I had never done such physical work in my life but I was ready to undergo anything. I would start at home, stop at my friend's house, change the attire to a poor sweeping lady and then go to the pharmaceutical company on the public bus. I sincerely did all the chores and would do extra cleaning right from the beginning so the manager and supervisor would be happy with me.

I suggested them things to clean up after regular work. In this way I got access to file stack and other important places where I couldn't go otherwise. I chalked out important sections of documents which could be helpful in giving me a clue. I also stealthily noted how the drugs were being manufactured and supplied from that place.

I quickly photocopied documents and treasury statements for later study. I also installed keyloggers secretly on the computers in the office to note what they were typing and passwords to various accounts.

I collected drugs and sent them for chemical analysis. After all the employees left the office, I would break in and continue my research as I earned the right for safekeeping of the keys, from the supervisor.

I collected the CCTV footage from the hard drives to check if Ankit had been to this place. According to Tanmay, Ankit had told that he had an idea about this. I spent all the time I could get into going through the footage. I mainly checked the outside cameras. Finally, I got a lead.

Just a few days before his death, Ankit had parked his bike outside and stealthily entered from the back window of the company to prevent himself from getting caught by the guards. It was dead of the night, so the security was not as tight outside, they were sleeping. He was seen going out after almost five hours after he went in. I suspected whether the owner of the company had any relationship with Ankit's murder.

I was determined as to not give up my research before I got hold of the killers.

Today was Sunday, No office. No hard work. I was cozying up on the bed as mother said, "Aarya, please get these things quickly from the market", mother handed down a list of items.

As I went to the market, I saw, there were varieties of Rakhis everywhere. Raksha Bandhan was approaching. My mother had explained the meaning of this festival to me long back, *'the sister ties a thread on her brother's wrist which symbolizes her love for him and the brother assures safety and protection for his sister.'*

Just looking at those rakhis, memories of my sweet brother clouded my mind and I couldn't stop the tears.

I missed him so much.

I decided to write a letter to him again on the day of Raksha Bandhan.

Dear Ankit,

Not even a day goes by without missing you. Your memories flock with no notice, frequently, unabated even after months of your departure. Sometimes you appear in my in dreams too.

You have no clue how much I miss you.

When you were a toddler, I took you to every other place on my tiny shoulders. Your naughty pranks and our petty quarrels are all that I have as a most valuable possession of my childhood memories.

When I left home for my studies, I came back to be with you on every *Rakhi* festival. It would be one of the most special days of the year for me. I would be counting the days when the festival was nearby. This festival gave me an opportunity to renew our relationship and feel the joy of being your sister.

The separation between us made this festival even more special for us. You were such a good brother. One year on this occasion, you had been abroad with Papa. Do you remember that I'd written a letter to you at that time? The ink got faint, with tears here and there.

As years passed by, you got caught up in addiction. It changed you so much. It affected your body, mind, your relationships, your career aspirations, everything. You started lying, stole money and sometimes were violent, we knew you were helpless and you hated it too.

I silently cried countless tears because I knew if you came to know this, you would feel ashamed and sorry. Please believe me; I have forgiven you for everything from the bottom of my heart. Your behavior hurt me sometimes but I always tried to mend my heart.

And then, suddenly, you were no more for us, forever, and my heart is broken, beyond repair, forever.

Recently I enquired for a solution to my suffering in your absence to an old priest. He looked tranquil and exalted. He said in his silvery voice that I need not suffer because you still exist somewhere beyond our reach. But I could reach you through my prayers. I asked the priest, what should I pray for you? Since I no more knew what you need and where you were. He said, pray to God, "Give him the strength to follow God's will and withstand the fleshly temptations and doubts in mind. It is the best prayer for anybody you can do". Since then, every day, I have been praying for you.

In your absence, my love for you has grown even more. Some people say this is the pinnacle of love when there are no personal expectations in it and there is only desire to serve and please the beloved. Although I am in pain without you, I am blessed with the opportunity to love you without any personal motives, selflessly.

You see, after your departure, I have understood your value even more.

This Rakhi festival, I promise you to try my best to find the culprits who have taken you away from my life and fight the menace of addiction. Although you are not here anymore, your memories are forever sealed in the vault of my heart. I promise to become a better person and a better daughter. I will take care of our parents in your absence.

Yours,

Aarya

The Walkathon

It had been more than a month now that I came out of the rehabilitation center. The memories of the place were still afresh. We were viewed there with respect as an individual, not as an addict who would be looked down upon. We were treated as sincere people who were trying their best to overcome addiction.

It was much different from the rest of the world where addicts were seen as abominations than people with abominable habits. This perspective mattered so much. I realized what an addict needed was love and acceptance in the society which will help him give up addiction sooner than never. If society kept alienating the addicts, they would never want to come in the mainstream. The dark side of a person thrives in darkness. I feel where there are no meaningful relationships based on love, healthy justified expectations, forgiveness and hope it's a dark world for them out there. Fortunately, I found it, so I could deal with my addiction.

While casually going through the newspapers one quiet afternoon, a particular clipping caught my attention,

'Walkathon against addiction- come and join'.

It was an advertisement regarding a walkathon event which was organized to collect funds and express solidarity against addiction. I already had a desire to join an organization working on the de-addiction program. I decided to meet the organizers to volunteer along with them for this cause.

I went through the newspaper again and found out the contact number for the organization. I called up and booked an appointment and reached the office before the appointed time.

It was an office in a posh apartment on the main road. The office had multiple educative panels about addiction. There were pictures highlighting important milestones of the organization on the wall. After reading those panels I learned that this organization had a chain of volunteers all over Maharashtra and they were conducting hundreds of activities throughout the year to spread awareness about addiction. I went to the person sitting in the office cabin.

He looked like he was one of the important people in the organization. There was a mid-aged man with gray-white hair. He was wearing baggy jeans and a simple blue checked shirt, untucked. He was working on the computer while he leaned on his comfortable chair, relaxed.

"Sir, I am Tanmay Bendale. I saw your advertisement regarding a walkathon event in the newspaper. I am keen on contributing to the cause of de-addiction. I want to join your organization and serve people. So I am particularly happy to see the walkathon ad and meeting you today. I would like to know how and when did you start your organization and how do you fight against addiction."

He said, "Our organization started about three decades ago and the founding members in the opening ceremony said that *Let this organization be reduced year after year to be closed one day.'* Unfortunately, even after three decades, we still exist. It indicates the increasing need of an organization in the society for de-addiction."

I was interested so I asked him, "Sir, I also wish to participate in de-addiction drives. What would it take to disenchant the younger generation from the fascination they feel from addiction?"

"I think Art-based awareness would be very useful."

"Sir what is this art based awareness?"

"It is a creative method of expression used for spreading awareness. It is educating people with creative arts, literature, drama, music etc. Scientific research has shown that better learning happens when multiple senses are used for learning. We need to creatively employ all available modalities of education for spreading the awareness. With the revolution of information sharing with social media, the attractiveness of the message can't be undermined. Nice short films, documentaries, attractive graphics which encourage people to stay away from the addiction at its very first are very important" he explained.

"Sir, what is the purpose for you to have

organized this walkathon specifically?"

"We have to encourage healthy substitutes for addiction just for engaging our mind. Exercise, skill development, learning various languages and spirituality are various solutions which can help a person to specifically stay away from the demon of addiction.

I recently read in some scientific journal that studying new languages or meeting new people release the same amount of dopamine in the brain which gets released while snorting drugs or consuming alcohol.

When you're getting the same amount of pleasure by indulging in activities favorable to your life, why not do it to get rid of an addiction? Once you find a meaningful goal in your life, the emptiness goes away. The healthy goals for purposes which are greater than one's own self encourage people to not give in to addiction. The purpose of this walkathon is also to raise fund, spread awareness against addiction and show solidarity for the same."

I was inspired by their cause. I said, "I would like to volunteer for you". After a discussion, it was decided that I and Aarya would be part of the organizing team for the walkathon to help them reach more public.

We started our walkathon at around 7 am in the morning. The participation response that the NGO got was overwhelming. School going kids, college students, corporate people, retired ones;

housewives etc. so many people participated in the marathon, our efforts to do publicity had been successful.

The plan was also to raise funds to support the awareness programs and rehabilitation center, the volunteers were busy since morning making arrangements for the 10km walkathon. There was a beautiful pandal at the start and the end of the venue. There were refreshments and drinks on the way. People were enthusiastic bringing in healthy vibes by just being there. And in just one day, around 3 lakh rupees were raised. We had arranged a program at the end of the walkathon.

There were a few guest speakers at the event. At first, one of the most distinguished school principals, Dr. Iqbal Pathan spoke. He had a thin white beard and a skull cap on his head. He looked like a devoted person. He had more than thirty-five years of teaching experience and he was known for his vast knowledge in youth psychology. He had won multiple awards and accolades for his teaching, innovations and educational development work. He rose with grace and went to the dais.

He started with sharing his experiences with students who had faced drug problems, "Many people think that using drugs is a sign of bravado and it adds to their personality. But in our experience, the people who drink or smoke are emotionally very weak. Resorting to intoxication to get away from dealing with their problems is a sign of weakness. Addicts face inferiority complex because of the guilt accumulated in their hearts."

He cleared his throat, and continued,

"To say 'No' to drugs, it needs more strength than saying yes to it.

The 'No' to drugs could come from thoughts like *'I do not like alcohol'*, or it could come as an obligation to other people like *'my parents have told me not to smoke'*, or it could come from our feelings such as, *'I do not feel like smoking'*. But the best 'No' come when there is a commitment for a higher purpose in your life.

The belief that, *'My body is a gift for a higher purpose of serving- entirely and I don't want to impair it even a bit, so I won't touch these intoxicants'*, this gives you a better way of saying 'No'. You are not denying somebody because of your ego or your inconvenience or your feelings but because you're living your life for a higher purpose and no power in the world has the right to distract you from that purpose. This strategy will help you to sort out many things in your *Zindagi*, by that I mean your life."

After a long pause, he continued ahead, "We need to commit ourselves for the welfare of all humans in this divine country. A nation full of insane druggards can't achieve its cherished dreams. The only priority in the life of an addict is his next dose, then where is the priority for Allah, country, family, society or the world?

The people who take shelter of drugs hobble to take their decisions while they become slow in assembling their thought processes and become retarded in their cognition."

I really liked this man's logic. Everything he spoke made sense to me.

"The cat shuts her eyes when somebody comes to beat her up or the ostrich buries his head in the ground when he sees a predator but these tactics do not save them, it makes them even more susceptible to their adversaries.

Similarly, the more one tries to do away from their troubles and sorrows by taking intoxicants, the stronger is the hold of the drugs over that particular person. That's all I have to say today, I wish you all a happy and healthy life ahead", everyone applauded him for the speech and appreciated his wisdom.

The next speaker was Mr. Jay Prakash. In the last 12 years, he had transformed his village into an intoxication free village and had built an organization which worked on making villages self-sustainable. He was the youngest Sarpanch in his village when he started at 26.

They had worked out projects such as complete waste-management, mechanical power generation by a windmill, water conservation, solar energy, quarrel-free village etc. Although he passed out as an engineer from a prestigious college in the city and having a high paying job, he had chosen to work in his village.

His village had become one of the most ideal villages in the country.

He started, "In our villages, people say Lord Shiva himself consumes weed so when it comes to us, why are we restricted? Lord Shiva drank poison from the ocean, so will you be able to do that too? Lying, cheating, stealing, robbing, gambling, gaming, having excessive sex urges and indulgences all these are corollaries of addiction. Please hear carefully and understand, it's not a casual act but a serious entrance into a path which is filled with thorns, for us and our kith and kins."

The atmosphere became serious and the attendees appeared to extend their focus.

"Youth has a rebellious tendency. They want to go against the old ideas, concepts etc. It's a thrill to them; the feeling of being unorthodox is something they think would make them look cool and attractive to others of their age."

With great emphasis, he said, "I request you to use your rebel against various evils still present in the society. Rather than dealing with fake problems on your screens deal with real problems faced by society. There are more NGOs in India than police stations. There is an NGO in India for every 600 people. Many of them need support in terms of manpower, funding, skills etc.

Many of you are students studying various professional courses, why can't we think of doing a summer/winter internship with such types of NGOs. It will give you plenty of professional experience which will help you in your career and at the same time, you will get immense satisfaction of selflessly working for a higher cause.

One such team of young people I know have created a mobile application, 'volstory'. It helps you find out volunteering opportunities which match your skill sets and which are near to you, it even helps you find volunteers if you want to take a social service initiative."

He was practically pleading the attendees to get up and do something about the current situation of the broken youth in this country, "So take advantage of such technological support systems to solve the problems around you. The opportunities are endless; we need to take advantage of those opportunities to spread good deeds around."

His talk was followed by the chief guest's speech.

The chief guest was the commissioner of police, Mrs.Thorat. She was a strong lady known in the city for her fearless approach against crimes. She addressed the event attendees,

"Dear participants, I thank you for participating in this marathon. I am happy to see such a huge number of people gathered at this place against the cause of drug de-addiction. At this time, we are facing a grim reality regarding drugs. A new study has found that opioids worth Rs 7,500 crore are consumed in Punjab annually. Of these, heroin's share is a towering Rs 6,500 crore.

And about 75%, it's the youth that is addicted to drugs. In India, 3.3 million deaths occur in a year because of alcohol consumption. A startling revelation has been made, that almost all the heroin that comes to Punjab is through the foreign elements facilitated by some rotten eggs in our own Border Security Force.

The borders of India are porous and the foreign elements take full advantage of this to push drugs inside the country. Punjab and Haryana are at a complete grip of this drug menace to the point that at least one person in every family is in the clutches of addiction. The weed addiction has become rampant in the Indian youth. People become lethargic and dull by consuming an excess of marijuana. We should take on the responsibility to weed out these weeds.

We have strict laws to deal with addiction. If you are caught using it or peddling to a client, you will land up behind the bars and then you will be dealt with sternly.

Many people ask about, what the police and the armed forces are doing? It's a huge city compared to which we have a couple of inspectors and then some more working under them in the anti-narcotics department. It's impossible to operate well when we're so shorthanded on the manpower. Even without it, it should be an individual responsibility to make sure the law and order are well maintained around. When you see somebody smoking in the non-smoking zone, it is your duty to remind that person that it is not a proper place for smoking and he should do it elsewhere.

What might happen if you did speak like that?

He may revolt and he may speak some abusive words to you. But once you do so, you will see that the crowd has already begun gathering around to support you.

It is true that 'You *have to take this initiative personally if you want to see more impact of these things.*' After all, someone has to stand up and lead.

I thank you again for assembling here; I wish you the best in your efforts to fight against the menace of addiction in the world."

Everyone applauded loudly as she walked away from the mic.

Mr. M. Srivastava, the director of 'Derby Lab and Co.' and family friend of Aarya along with Mr. Mandar, were present for the function. Through their hands, we distributed the gifts and certificates to winners and participants of the walkathon.

We met Mr. M. Srivastava after the function. A pudgy man in his forties had an expressionless face and dark brown skin with a light spot on his chin.

"How are you? Seeing you after many days." He asked Aarya.

"I am somehow carrying on my life. It has not been very long since Ankit has passed away. "

He spoke in a sympathetic, grave voice, "I was so sorry to hear Mandars departure. Life sometimes takes us on difficult, rough terrains. Navigating our way through such terrains could be a challenging and daunting task. But it is said difficult roads often lead to beautiful destinations. I wish that you come out of this rough period with more maturity and wisdom. Please let me know if I could help you in some way."

Pointing out to Mr.Mandar who was standing near him, he explained how Mandar has achieved great success while passing through great struggle during his research., Mandars life and success was an example for entire country. I acknowledged this with a appreciative glance and smile which he acknowledged politely.

While we were in the discussion, police Commissioner Mrs. Thorat ma'am joined us.

She said, "I thank you for your part of organizing a team and gathering public for this marathon. We need more intelligent people like you. Now the drug menace is getting circulated all over the internet as well. Earlier we used to get leads from our local spy network and we would catch the culprits. But recently we have come to know that drug peddling had spread over the internet via the dark web which we are not able to track yet. There is the possibility of having such a network in this city too. And we must hunt it down."

"Madam, we have some important leads regarding addictions spread over the dark web."

I shared our suspicions on Ankit's death and our investigation trail up to the pharmaceutical unit that was manufacturing the drugs. She appeared to be amazed at our research but apprehensive about our security. When I revealed the identity of the owner of the company, she curled her face. She explained that the owner had links with top politicians and it was not easy to just catch him. He had quite a lot of political connections and a good amount of money he'd use for such causes. He could easily avail a number of lawyers at his disposal to help him with a case. We had to gather substantial evidence if we wanted to catch him. Even Aarya said that she wanted some more time to finish her investigation and consolidate all the evidence, few of the reports she had sent for investigation were pending.

Finish Her Off

It was almost midday. The sun was emitting fire. The rusty tin roof above our heads did nothing to reduce the effect of the sun. The fan did all but funnel the dry air which gave no relief from the heat outside in our tiny 200 sq. feet room.

The chawl had labyrinths, shooting ranges, and the secret ways from the kitchen which opened directly out which made this chawl almost invincible from situations of sudden raids. I always had a guard standing outside.

We were hiding in one of the chawls in Dharavi. Inside, humans were almost crammed together in that finite space.

My phone rang rather loudly, or maybe it was the little space that we were crammed into that the phone sounded even louder. It was Sameer across the phone.

"Hello, Hana Ma'am? There's some bad news."

"What happened?"

"The confidentiality of our production plant has been breached."

"Who's that traitor? Is he an employee there."

"Yes. *She* acted like an employee."

He told me of how a girl disguised as an employee had been stealing information. He was a supervisor there at the same time he worked for us unknown to Mr. Aggrawal. He received the information about her forgery from one person.

"Do not just sack her from the job but finish that traitor before anybody comes to know of it. Do it quietly. I do not want to take any risk."

"Yes, ma'am".

"I will wait for the news of your success."

It took plenty of years for us to come this far and finally, we were this close to fulfilling our destiny. I didn't want to take any risk. It had taken so many years of patience and planning. I had been helplessly waiting for this day to come.

In my college, I came across my brothers from across the border. They quickly identified with my plans. They fanned my desire for revenge. Hafiz bhai was the chief among them. He was a mastermind and knew history so well.

He explained to me how I was on such an important task and probably chosen by 'Allah' for this mission.

I was waiting for a call, regarding the success of our mission.

Tempt Fate

I looked in the mirror while brushing my teeth in the morning. My skin was tanned by working on the premises of my office under the sun and I had become leaner. My palms had become harder, dry and cracked. I didn't know how long it was going take to continue like this to find out details related to Ankit's murderers.

I went to the pharmaceutical company office as usual. I did the daily assigned cleaning work. By evening all the people left the office. There were guards outside the office. I switched on the computer.

While I was entering the password, I was suddenly surrounded by three muscular men. All of them were masked. One of them had a revolver in his hand. One of them grabbed me from my back and twisted my hand. The other pointed a gun at my forehead "What are you doing in here?"

"No, Sirji, nothing. I was just curious about this machine. I wanted to learn it so I switched it on. Nowadays everyone should learn com...pu...ter." I somehow formed a coherent sentence.

"You fool; do you think we don't know who you are? You have been fooling us for months, noting down all activities going down here and accessing all documents. You're caught and this won't continue anymore because you're gonna die. Any last words before we execute you?"

I was aghast. I wasn't expecting this. They knew my disguise. I was left with no option. Three powerful men and one with a revolver at my forehead, my chances of escaping from their hold were bleak. I repented. I should have been more careful, how could I be caught in this state. Thoughts of my parents crossed my mind. They didn't know what I'd been doing all this time. I was their only hope after Ankit. I couldn't imagine how they would survive if I weren't there.

So I begged for forgiveness, asked them to let me go.

"Please leave me. I will not tell anyone anything. Please forgive me."

"You will be pardoned only in heavens. God may be merciful to you but not us," saying this he slapped me and pushed me far into a corner of the room. I looked back as he was about to pull the trigger but suddenly two people stormed in. They were armed and had masks on. One of them fired, as the bullet punctured the muscular man's head, the gun fell from his grasp and he collapsed on the floor with a thud. Blood squirted everywhere. The rest of them ran for their lives. These people released me.

The police commissioner had assigned two people to go undercover and work along with me in the company in case things went wrong. I couldn't thank her enough to keep me safe.

In a short time, we collected all the drug

samples present there and I copied as much data as possible. It was risky to work thereafter. After chemical analysis, we found the lab owner guilty of producing, storing and distributing the narcotics. We filed a case against him. The factory was sealed.

On the very next day, police caught the lab owner and the court sent him into police custody for the following couple of weeks.

Mrs.Thorat, the police commissioner, shared their interrogation details in the custody with us.

They asked him, "How did you get into this drug business?"

"Sorry, sir. The money blinded me, I made through it. I wanted to expand my business, and I wanted quick capita, free from interest rates. So I joined this business."

"Who gave you the secrets about the processes for manufacturing these drugs?"

"Sir, there's a lady, she met me in my office and knew my whole background. I had a factory, but it was in a loss and I was desperate to make money. I had evaded tax for two years. She knew all the loopholes. She offered to help me in my business for making quick money. I had to manufacture these drugs in my plant. She would get the drug formulas and do the marketing. I was hesitant, I knew it wasn't right, but to keep my money upright I took the chances and agreed. She created a network of hucksters for spreading these drugs. Our poor Indian boys once hooked to weed and substance couldn't think of anything else but the next dose. She supplied drugs completely free of cost for those who got maximum customers."

"Who is this lady you're talking of?"

"Sir, I don't know her name. I came to know of her address from one of our drivers when they once dropped her. She stays in a chawl in Dharavi."

The owner gave the detailed address of the lady.

The police raided her house on the address but the house was empty. After short investigation police found out somebody had just left the house. It was in a small chawl in Dharavi, Mumbai. The room was small and stuffed. There were various quotations in Urdu marked on the walls.

We had failed, she had probably escaped. It confused us as to how we were supposed to track her down now that she had escaped.

She used applications for communication which would keep her identity anonymous. We inquired from the other residents in the chawl but nobody knew about her. She always covered herself with a burka so nobody saw her face which meant we were losing our leads to this case.

We again inquired from Mr. Aggrawal.

Mr. Aggrawal explained that he would transfer the money using bitcoin. We only had the bitcoin address at our avail. We planned to meet Mr. Indraveer Singh who was one of the very reputed cybersecurity experts in India.

We went to his office in the city. He was known

for his no-nonsense attitude, with his jet black hair and his eyes brown and piercing, he commanded awe. Hailing from Uttar Pradesh, he had a facile tongue with a touch of royalty. He was famous for his expertise in internet security domain and high morals.

We explained the whole matter to him. He was kind and sympathetic towards us.

He told us, "Bitcoin is a cryptocurrency which was unregulated by any government and was generally used for online transactions since nobody could track it. So many of the illegal transactions happen over the internet using bitcoin for money transfers."

We asked him, was it possible to trace the lady since we only had her bitcoin address with us?

He pondered over it for a while and then answered, "Bitcoin is pseudonymous. Sending and receiving bitcoins is like writing under a pseudonym- a fictitious name. If an author's pseudonym is ever linked to their identity, everything they ever wrote under that pseudonym will now be linked to them. In Bitcoin, your pseudonym is the address to which you receive Bitcoin. If she has not used her bitcoin address in any other place then it would be difficult to trace her out. But if the bitcoin address has been shared over the internet for payment or fund collection purpose, etc. Then it gets tagged to that website and eventually a person who is running the website, so in this way, we can track down that person."

We shared the bitcoin address with him. He did some online search.

After a while, the address got flagged.

"And here it is...... there was the same bitcoin address on one website of welfare trust for collecting donations."

The name of the owner was shown as Hana Sheikh. It seemed that she was running a welfare trust and skill training courses for students and she was collecting donations for it.

We checked the name of the institute she ran, on the Foreign Contribution Regulations Act (FCRA) portal. On this portal, we have all the information about all the trusts registered for collecting foreign donations.

After checking her FCRA account from the bank, it was found that she had regularly received huge sums of money from the Middle East. She might have also been involved in a few terror funding activities.

We issued a notice to all the banks to submit all the account details of all the people with a name of Hana Sheikh and who lived in Mumbai as well as the account details of the welfare trust.

We collected all the statements. The money was gathered from foreign countries in the name of the welfare trusts and was being transferred to Kashmir.

It was clear that she was an intelligent lady and

had excellent managerial skills but, she misused all her knowledge, such an intelligent mind guided in the wrong direction, I wondered what the cause was.

We planned a raid on the welfare trust run by her. She ran a religious school there. We surveyed the place before raiding. She was definitely coming there regularly. There were about fifteen young adults who attended that program regularly.

There were two guards in civil disguise that would guard that place in shifts. We noted their timings.

The Plot

I was anxious to hear from Sameer, the outcome of the operation. The traitor must not go alive. We couldn't afford a single mistake. India's anti-terrorist squad and Narcotics Control Bureau were very active and a small mistake would completely disrupt our plans.

I was looking at my phone constantly to get the good news; at last, he called me up.

"What happened Sameer? Have they neutralized the target?"

"Hana Ma'am, there's bad news."

"What happened, you useless rascals? It has become difficult to trust you."

"Ma'am, we had almost caught the target and held her captive. We were just about to knock her off, but the unknown gunmen stormed in, I believe they were police. Before our agent could shoot the target, the cops shot him. The other two people fled away."

"Did he survive? Did he spill out our identities?"

"Fortunately ma'am he died on spot and revealed nothing about us. Ma'am, I am afraid. I think the security forces have smelled something foul with us and we are being intercepted. We are being tracked. We need to change the location."

"You fool. You always make mistakes. How

would I vindicate myself in-front of Hafiz Bhai and the others? Do you have an idea of how hard I have worked to earn his trust?"

Our mission was important. We had been successful in establishing a team which was not only successful in slowly killing Indian kids through drugs but could also generate substantial funds for other terrorist activities. It was just the beginning of the plot. We would not stop unless we completed our revenge.

We changed our location of the stay immediately. I decided not to come out of the residence at least one week. Next week I went to welfare trust. As I entered the office, there was a couple of police in civil disguise already waiting for me. They quickly grabbed me and flipped me in their car and drove me to their headquarters.

I was under their radar now under chargers of having run a drug racket and funding terrorist activities.

They had caught me unsuspected.

They confiscated my mobile and laptop. They locked me up behind the bars.

By collecting information from the mobile, they quickly raided all the other places related to us.

I came to know from some guards who were conversing with each other. They wrecked those places, and they had raided simultaneously twelve places across the country in a short time.

They came to know about our cross border connections. They collected the material with which we used to train our people; they called this 'radicalization'. They also found ammonium nitrate, potassium nitrate, mobiles, sim cards, alarm clocks, electric wires, etc. Our plans of major bomb attack blasted away. They had caught our whole team in various states of India. We were in serious trouble now.

My plans were all jeopardized. My future had disappeared into thin air. The Commissioner of police, Mrs.Thorat came to meet me in my cell. Everyone knew her for her knowledge and discipline although she was also kind and understanding.

"We have found objectionable content in your mobile; you were in touch with terrorists across the border. There are inflammatory videos, seditious messages you have exchanged in your mobile. You will be prosecuted for the same. You cannot deny. We have caught your whole network with evidence. Rather it will be best for you now if you accept your mistakes and answer our questions truthfully. We have also caught your other colleagues and your whole module has been busted. We'd like to know why you did it."

"When I was a child, I had seen my parents being killed brutally in the Mumbai riots by some crooks. They did not bother to kill them in front from me.

I screamed out to the people to help my parents but my cries disappeared in the air. I became an orphan in front of my own eyes.

The burning pain inside demanded revenge, I couldn't afford to forgive. The scar was too deep. I tried to find who could help me, anywhere and everywhere."

"I am really sad about that incident. I wish to ask you now, have you never experienced kind behavior from a person from other religion?"

"I have...but,"

"Have you not seen egoistic, violent people in your own religion? The people for whom you are working in their country, although they belong to the same religion, there is always some form of internal communal riot going on. What about Afghanistan? What about Syria? At these places too, so many innocent beings are being killed. Have you ever thought about that? It's not the religion; it's about people who perform such things in the name of religion. Selfish people find ways even to use religion for their own selfish purposes"

"You are right, but I was concerned with my own personal loss."

"So you want to destroy thousands of lives for losing your few dear ones. We sympathize for what has happened to you and the killers of your parents should be punished hard by law but your actions are not justifiable."

"I never thought from your point of view. Actually, my feelings were hurt and the childhood memories left me with burnt feelings. I could never deal with those horrible memories and I thought if somehow, I could take revenge then it would make the pain go away. My cross-border instructors nurtured this thought. They fed me with even more violent videos and articles. My conscience told me that there might be something wrong in what I was doing but they gave me references from scriptures. I learned in Quran that Allah is the one God and to those who adore him, Allah will redeem them but others would be doomed. It was a sacred mission."

Mrs. Thorat replied, "Allah means the omnipotent creator, the God. There can be only one God across many religions but he could be referred by multiple names. You call him 'Allah- The all-powerful', somebody may call 'Jehovah' which means true, supreme and eternal one and somebody may call him 'Ishwar'- Supreme Controller. People call the name of God based on their own culture and personal realization. There are good as well as bad people across all the religions. Even in the religion, I practice, there are people who misuse it for their ulterior motives. We have to come above such differences.

Now the court will decide your fate, all that I spoke of right now was because I believe you have been misguided and your previous impressions have not been properly handled to calm you.

We have also found confidential and classified research information from your laptop and mobile. You have got these files stolen from 'Derby Research Lab'. Your conversations on social media and chatting applications show that you were intimately associated with a famous young scientist Mr. Mandar Sahastrabuddhe. You have gradually lured him and put him under your net for stealing the research information. This research has been sold to Mr. Aggrawal for manufacturing drugs and it has been sent across the border. "

"Do you agree to have done this?"

I remained silent. I was cursing my destiny, rather, I was cursing the choices made by me which had taken their course and put me in a serious predicament such as this. The anger had become the cause of my downfall.

Who is the Murderer?

Aarya asked me, "Tanmay, how long it will take to find the killer."

I had no clue. As time passed by, we were desperate for the news and it made us all restless. Yet there were no clues about Ankit's death.

Neither Mr. Aggrawal nor Hana had shown any connection with Ankit's death when they were being interrogated by the police. Both their statements had no mention of Ankit as if they were not aware of him at all. We too had no positive leads in this case. I thought maybe after we got the scientist under arrest, he would give us information which would give us a lead to solving Ankit's murder.

We suspected the scientist for the death of Ankit. Ankit had received lead about drug research information leakage from Derby Labs which he wanted to share with them. Mandar had access to and possession of all the confidential files. He might have feared that after this news become public, he will be held responsible for the whole thing, in this fear he might have killed Ankit. So it was important to catch him at any cost.

After they searched Hana's mobile, it showed innumerable pictures of them together. Hana's social media sites history also showed evidence of how she had lured him in.

Hana was thoroughly interviewed. I had seen her when she was caught, she was gorgeous. Her blond highlight hair was put together beautifully in a chignon. Her teeth were like a row of white pearls. With a raised, pointed nose, chocolate brown eyes, the Cupid's-bow red lips surrounded her small mouth, she had an attractive bust. Everything perfect. She looked like an angel, the handcuffed angel. No wonder she was chosen for honey trapping Mandar by Hafiz.

She had been stalking Mandar's profile on social media for a very long time. Mandar was a regular trekker; she joined his trekking group and followed him on such events. Met him in the journey, convinced him that it was a coincidence that she was there and sweet-talked him infiltrating his thoughts as well.

Befriending him with a warm smile and sweet words, she advanced their friendship. From texting occasionally to every day, they happened to share a good bond. Mandar proved an easy target for her. Very soon he was like her pet. It was as if she controlled him and fished out all the information either directly or indirectly. They became close and he shared his office matters with her as well. She paid a short visit to him at his place too. He wanted intimacy from her but she pushed him off with the promise of marriage.

Gradually his infatuation with her led him to reveal all the secrets to her. She managed to steal the rest of the documents out of his personal computer when he was unaware. It gave her access to all the drug formulas; they had worked on. Their company had created versions of chemical drugs while doing experiments which were cheaper to produce but had a better drug trip and also important drugs to counter biological warfare.

There was an immediate arrest warrant for Mandar.

When the police approached Mandar, to arrest him, he had already eloped from his residence. He was a bachelor, staying as a paying guest in Borivali. He probably escaped after hearing the news about Hana's arrest. Police tried all possible means to nab him but he was nowhere to be found. He was the last suspect who could be involved in Ankit's murder.

One week passed. It seemed as if we had reached a dead end. We wondered if he had left the country somehow.

"Tanmay, how should we go ahead? There is no clue of Mandar, the suspect has run away", Aarya said.

I was worried too, "The police have tried all possible means, and I suspect he might have flown out of India."

Aarya said, "The police have already issued a

notice to all the airports to detain him immediately as soon as he is detected.”

I said, “Then even he has to run away with forged documents, it will take some time, but in this case, we are really running out of time.”

“I suspect he is being helped by Hana’s aides.”

I excused myself for an hour. Whenever I was unclear, indecisive, I chose to go away and think over various solutions. This really worked for me. After a while, I came back to her.

I saw her frown and told her, “We can try tracking the peddler’s bike in which we had put GPS machine, it is still there.”

Aarya replied, “I completely forgot about the bike. While working at the company unit I came to know the bike actually didn’t belong to the peddler but it was used by different people to peddle drugs. Later it was never to be seen again.”

We checked the whereabouts of the bike. It was parked in some remote part of the city in the basement of an apartment. We informed the police and they decided to raid the place. Fortunately, because of our good relations with Police and our involvement in this case, we were receiving all the updates about the police operation.

Mrs. Thorat assigned the police team led by Inspector Irfan Sheikh and Inspector Advait Raut.

Irfan was chosen because of his knowledge of

Urdu which was imperative as the messages were in Urdu and Advait was an expert in the anti-terrorist squad.

After the reconnaissance of the place, they realized that there were some suspicious activities going on- The place was visited frequently by a couple of masked bikers. Based on their movement it appeared that there might be some armed men inside. Mandar was found in the gallery talking on his mobile phone.

The Police planned a 'cordon and kick operation' to enter inside and it was decided that Advait would lead the cordon team while Irfan would lead the team which would storm inside the house. At night, Irfan and his team raided the house and entered by force. There were total of four gunmen inside. They opened fire and in retaliation, the police also began firing their guns and thus ensued a fierce gun-battle. After an hour, two gunmen were shot by the police- one died on the spot and the other one was captured alive. The remaining gunmen, along with Mandar tried to flee the scene but were eventually captured by the police.

They were taken into custody and after their grilling; they revealed that they were radicalized in Kerala. Hana had recruited them under the guidance of Hafiz who instructed them to provide shelter and security to Mandar.

In the interrogation of Mandar, it was revealed that after the news about Hana's arrest and

Mandar's involvement with her spread all over, Mandar decided to quit the country for better future prospects. However, he found it impossible for him to leave the nation on his own since now everyone was aware and there were already arrest warrants in his name. That time, he was contacted by Hana's aides and they promised him to take him to Dubai via a private jet. He didn't want to be part of them but it was important for him to first leave the country. They took him to their shelter while his fake documents were being made for travel outside India.

Mandar was full of regret. His plans were shattered. He had no clue who she was. She wasn't Hana for him, she'd taken the name 'Rina Gupta' in order to lure him in- the one-time hero for a nation of who had led a team to invent useful drugs for the army and air force had succumbed to the charms of a traitor. It reminded me of the story of the elephant catching in earlier times from the book shared by Jim. To catch a male elephant, people used a female elephant. They dug a big hole in the ground to capture the elephant in it and covered the hole. When a male-elephant spotted his female, he would seek her company and advance towards her thereby falling into the trap that had been designed for him. Similarly, Mandar had fallen victim to lust because of Hana and put in jail for his offense of carelessly sharing confidential information related to national security.

Later, Mrs. Thorat called us for a private

meeting with her. "Congratulations Tanmay and Aarya. Because of your great support we could bust this whole drug racket and also nab the people who breached confidential information related to national security."

"Thank you, madam; we are really inspired by your simplicity and professionalism." There wasn't much else I could say to her anyway.

"I am aware that you can't be happy unless you find the truth behind Ankit's death."

Aarya replied, "Yes madam, it is my mission."

Mrs. Thorat commented, "In the case of homicide, the chief motives are usually lust, money, love and even honor. If we can filter out the main incentive, we could pinpoint who could be the primary suspect for Ankit's murder. Certainly not the peddler since he was his good pal and there was no monetary motive involved. If you think about the owner of the factory, Mr. Aggrawal; he was abroad when Ankit had sneaked into his factory and even when he was killed. This eliminates him as a suspect. The same can be said for Hana as she also never knew Ankit.

The remaining suspicion falls on Mandar. He could be the killer but his fingerprints do not match those at the crime scene. If we go by financial consideration, Mandar did not have any financial stakes in this whole drug invention and production business since he was just a scientist working as an employee at Derby Labs. He did not hate Ankit; so did he kill him because Ankit came to know about his relationship with Hana, and feared his secret would be out in public? Even then, it is not possible because Mandar had no idea about Hana's real identity till the news of her arrest was spread all over."

"Then who is the killer? "I demanded exasperatedly.

Commissioner Mrs. Thorat cleared her throat, "I definitely suspect some high ranking person from Derby Labs."

"How could you be so obvious about this?"

"Because the reputation and net worth of Derby Labs were at stake had Ankit revealed to the public the breach of confidentiality. They could have lost the big contracts which would have hampered their business massively. Since Ankit did not intend to share his findings at the factory with the police department, there remains only somebody from the Derby lab."

"It seems logical what you say. But how do we narrow it down from hundreds of employees to one?"

"I checked the financial transaction details of all the top ranking people and investors of Derby Labs"

"And?"

"I suspect Mr. M. Srivastava himself."

"What?! He is our family friend. He is known for his hard work to reach to the top of his company and he is also known for his philanthropy. Why should he do this? What evidence do you have?"

"He sold his a major portion of shares just after a day of Ankit's death. Derby Labs were making a great profit and had great deals then why should he sell off his major chunk of shares. We also obtained the fingerprints of Mr. M. Srivastava from his office glass and it matched the fingerprints on the glass obtained on the crime scene.

Moreover, Aarya you had been attacked at the pharmaceutical factory. It was because, after walkathon, you revealed whole information about your disguise to Mr. M. Srivastava while you were telling it to me, he was just standing beside. Later he arranged through his agents to communicate this information to Hana so that she would kill you."

We had caught the killer.

Mr. Srivastava was called for an inquiry immediately. Initially, he thought it was regarding Mandar sharing the confidential information from Derby Labs.

"Sir, why did you sell a major chunk of your shares from Derby Labs a few months before?"

"I sold it as I had an alternative investment

plan.”

“But Derby Labs’ shares were rising during that time. Were you aware of the breach of confidentiality by Mr. Mandar?”

As he was being interrogated a cold sweat broke out on his forehead. He wiped his face, put up an easy-going expression and replied “I was not aware of it”

“Our information sources reveal that you were very well aware of this. We have checked Ankit’s and your mailbox. It reveals that you had planned a meeting earlier, and you did meet him at your office. Ankit knew this confidentiality leakage and you being MD of the company and his family friend, he informed you this information without making it public even to his parents to save your reputation. You feared if this information goes public then you will face a backlash from investors and that’s why you sold your shares to save your money. You knew if the public comes to know of this leakage then your company’s shares would tank. That’s why you not only did sell your shares but also hid the news of the information leakage so that people should not doubt you selling shares as insider trading which could put you behind the bars. And just to maintain your shenanigans you murdered Ankit. You were afraid of either losing your money or facing criminal proceedings in case you were caught selling those shares”.

By this time he had become very tense. He tried

to push his stand. "Your allegations are slanderous and preposterous! I have sold my shares for a purely personal cause. You cannot prove this."

"You had arranged a party to celebrate the success of Derby Labs. You invited Ankit's parents to the event so that nobody should be there at his home except Ankit. Under the pretext of chest pain, you excused yourself from the party and went to hospital. But hospital records show, you never got admitted there. You went to Ankit's home without your mobile so nobody would track you later. Both of you must have had few pegs before he was completely intoxicated and vulnerable and that's when you injected the drug in the right arm. You cleaned up the surroundings. Although you washed your glass, it still left fragments of your fingerprints which we preserved. Do you know what we discovered? They perfectly matched with your fingerprints!

Mr. Srivastava, now what do you have to say? Do you admit you killed Ankit in cold blood? You heavily intoxicated him with alcohol till he was half-unconscious and overdosed him with drugs. Eventually, he died."

Mr. M. Srivastava fell silent. He had killed Ankit for his greed. We had found the actual killer at last. After all this hustle, it was finally resolved and we could all move on in peace.

'There are three gates leading to downfall- lust, anger, and greed.

I had been an alcohol addict and this addiction dictated my life. It was physical and gross. But the in case of all the culprits behind drug racket and Ankit's murder, the addiction to greed, anger, and lust was mental and subtle.

I could quickly realize the negative consequences of my addiction and I knew I was doing wrong somewhere which will produce harmful results for me but for these culprits, their addiction had made them blind to the consequences of their actions and they thought it was the best thing for them and they harbored these addictions to the degree that they were all caught in crime against other innocents.

I was fortunate to recognize the problem, get the company of people who helped me to get out of it but these people could never get the company of people who could guide them out of this.

Based on my little story, I can say that most of the people have some form of gross or subtle addictions. Unless we recover from these harmful patterns, we are bound to suffer. We need knowledge or expert guidance to find out these weeds and we need to weed out these addictions from our fertile hearts where seeds of love and compassion are supposed to grow.

****